Amy, I love you! You come from a position because you are so highly qualified that you expect that people are as highly qualified as you. Others can learn from you about how to find the right professional. So, they are not going to get crappy advice. We see bad advice all the time and you have to clean it up. She helps people, and owners build their businesses, and grow their businesses in ways that, well, frankly you may never have thought about. You are so detail oriented with what you do.

Ken Krell, Amazing Digital Events

Amy Herrick is a "ROCKSTAR" ! I absolutely loved having her as a guest on my podcast as well as on my live stream. She has so much value to give that having one conversation is not enough. I highly recommend Amy as a guest speaker, you will not be disappointed, but you will be amazed at her wealth of knowledge. Amy Rose is just amazing. She is great at what she does. She will help you build your business correctly with the right foundations.

Laquita Monley, La Quita's ToolBox Podcast

I love what you are doing. You have so much knowledge. I love finding people who have just a little bit of a different perspective on things because it makes you think. I've always kind of been questioning if the crowd is doing it, is it really right? I don't know. Is it a group thing? You have given me a ton of value.

Chris Gunkle , Unrivaled Experts

Whatever you got that involves detailed numbers, you will not find, in my estimate, a more thorough, careful, helpful hand. You cannot do better.

Artie Vipperla, Psychic Grandmaster, Energy Healer & Spiritual Guide

Self-Employed Taxes: Unleashing Schedule C Deductions

A Line-By-Line Guide to Unlock Deductions and Create New Tax Savings for Small Business Owners and Independent Contractors

Free Audio Version Included

Amy Rose Herrick

Profit-Building Specialist

International Best-Selling Author

Published by Amy Rose Herrick

Herrick, Amy Rose

Self-Employed Taxes: Unleashing Schedule C Deductions

A Line-By-Line Guide to Unlock Deductions and Create New Tax Savings for Small Business Owners and Independent Contractors

First edition

Christiansted, US Virgin Islands: Amy Rose Herrick

xii, 170 pages, 11 inches

Taxation | Self-employment |Tax planning | Independent Contractor |Sole Proprietor | Single Member LLC | Finances| Tax Deductions | Retirement Plans | Tax Preparation |Business Expenses |Home Office |

ISBN: 978-1-960427-23-6

LCCN 2023942651

336.2

Amy Rose Herrick's books may be purchased in bulk for premiums, groups, educational, business or sales promotional use. For information, please write to: Amy@AmyRoseHerrick.com.

DEDICATION

This book is dedicated to all the visionary entrepreneurs and business owners who dare to dream, take risks, and strive for greatness.

Your unwavering determination and relentless pursuit of success inspire us all.

This book is dedicated to you—the innovators, the creators, coaches, artists, teachers, solopreneurs, and the trailblazers—whose passion and resilience fuel the engine of progress.

May these pages serve as a guiding light on your entrepreneurial journey, empowering you to overcome challenges, embrace opportunities, and achieve your boldest aspirations.

Your dedication to making a difference in the world is a testament to the true spirit of entrepreneurship.

Thank you for being the driving force behind positive change, and for inspiring others to fearlessly pursue their dreams.

To access your free audio version, please use this link:

https://www.moneywithamyaudiobooks.com/self-employed-taxes-unleashing-schedule-c-deductions

CONTENTS

Introduction

Are you a self-employed Schedule C taxpayer? This book is specifically for you, or those who will be Schedule C filers as you become an entrepreneur.

Let me ask you pointed questions to help you see if you will benefit from this book.

Do you receive 1099's or other forms of payment including cash, checks, Stripe, PayPal, Zelle, credit cards, etc. to pay you for work you do as a self-employed person or gig worker?

Are you clueless when it comes to saving taxes consistently?

Do you need an easy step-by-step process to master tax planning?

Do you have the last three years of filed tax returns accessible for you to use for reference while reading this article?

Are you ready to learn this new money management lifetime benefiting your wallet skill?

Well, if you answered "yes" to any of the above five questions, you are in the right place, at the right time, for the right answers to the questions that you do not even know how, what, or where to ask! Keep reading!

Now let us ask more clarifying questions:

Can you list all the taxes your self-employment income may be subject to in your tax jurisdiction?

Can you list all the self-employed tax deductions you are entitled to easily?

Are you getting the most out of your tax advantages because of your unique business structure status?

Have you had a meaningful conversation with your tax professional to understand what tax advantageous deductions you are missing?

Do you have the last three years of filed tax returns accessible for you to use for reference while reading this material?

Well, if you answered "no " to any of the above five questions, you are in the right place for help.

I know you are busy.

I know you want answers right now, so keep reading.

We have forms and lines on forms to discuss in a brief time you may have never reviewed before.

I will make it as easy as possible for you.

I know you can do this with me by your side guiding you each step of the way.

I want you to know at this moment in your life, you hold more long-lasting financial power in your hands right now than you may realize.

It is time to get started.

CHAPTER 1

Types of Tax Preparers

MONEY WITH AMY SERIES

SELF-EMPLOYED TAXES:
Unleashing Schedule C Deductions

This book is written from my decades of experience assisting self-employed professionals at every level of entrepreneurship from the spark of an idea before a step is taken to be an entrepreneur, to entrepreneurs who have been in business for decades.

I am focusing on the Schedule C entrepreneur here exclusively.

You will often begin an entrepreneurial journey as a Schedule C taxpayer and grow into other structures like multi-partner LLC's or LLLP's, C corporations, S Corporations or even change into non-profits.

Others are best served staying as a Schedule C taxpayer and it works perfectly for your needs.

Please understand there are in my mind DISTINCT kinds of tax preparers:

Self-Preparers- These individuals use Turbo Tax, Free IRS websites and HR Block type tax preparation software programs to prepare their taxes thinking this is easy if I just answer prompts or questions because they believe doing it themselves will "save" them money. They ignore the cost of their time and the cost of missed deductions or incorrect data entry errors.

Taxpayers acting as preparers could be right.

They could be very wrong too.

Volunteers: There are community groups that offer only free extremely basic tax prep for quite simple tax situations around springtime.

Taxpayer may have only one or two W2's, a Social Security or pension tax form, very minor forms that need compiled and filed.

These community volunteers are not there to answer complex tax questions or give more than the basic tax guidance and fill out the most basic tax forms.

It is a free community service.

Only the most basic tax filers benefit from these programs.

Reactive Paid Preparers: These preparers, who may be doing taxes either within a firm or as part time gig like workers, design their tax practices to accept what data they receive from the taxpayer, compile the numbers on tax forms, hand them back with an invoice and they are done.

There is usually little discussion about the entries or missing entries.

They rarely ask questions.

They are not engaged in changing the results of putting the numbers on the page.

This works for taxpayers with simple situations.

This does not work for taxpayers who have no idea what is missing in their records submissions or what should be included in the records they submit.

Pro-Active Tax Preparers: These professionals ask probing questions no matter what data you provide.

They want you to verify items or provide additional information for clarity.

They converse with you using probing questions to help understand your unique resources, challenges, recordkeeping practices, business dynamics, etc.

They offer suggestions for specific actions to take to reduce tax liabilities, explaining why this would be a good move for you.

They help you improve recordkeeping to gain more tax deductions, project current and future tax liabilities for income and purchase planning reference.

They keep an eye on your tax brackets year to year to advise when it is best for you to add money to your retirement savings on a pre-tax or post-tax basis.

They suggest when you should convert taxable IRA or 401k like accounts to tax free Roth IRA or 401k Roth type accounts.

They advise you of new or upcoming tax law changes that may benefit you.

They do a tax projection every year to help you change W4 forms on W2 income and quarterly estimates when W4's does not apply.

You call them during the year to ask how to manage financial issues before you make costly mistakes.

This relationship does not work for taxpayers who are sloppy recordkeepers unwilling to learn to keep good records, or those who are trying to lie about their income or expenses.

This works for taxpayers who want to pay the least amount of taxes now and over a lifetime and taxpayers who want to be informed about how they can increase wealth over time.

Which of the types of preparers listed above are you using? Does it meet your true needs? Have you outgrown your current provider relationship as your tax situation has become more complex?

Let me tell you right now, I fall in the Pro-Active category. This book is written because I am tired of seeing so many taxpayers who are not being served to my level of service pay more in taxes than they need to year after year because they do not know their options.

Do you feel you are at a distinct disadvantage because you have no idea what questions you should be asking your preparer? Countless taxpayers feel the same way you do on the complexities of taxes they are required to file.

As a ripple effect, you have no idea what data you should be compiling for the lowest tax bills possible.

Then, as a final insult to injury, you have no idea the amount of additional taxes you are paying because of the communication breakdowns you think are normal.

Over a lifetime, you will pay tens, or hundreds of thousands of dollars in additional taxes, you never should have owed, had you been more informed about taxes and taxpayer opportunities and responsibilities.

I see that as money wasted that you earned you should have been able to keep.

That is why you are here. You want to learn how to be a more tax savvy entrepreneur.

So, let us start out showing you how I, with my boutique style tax practice as a reference point, help you identify the differences in services available to you when you think about the relationship that you have with your current tax preparer and what you want out of your tax preparation relationship.

I need to add a quick caveat the person who is doing your bookkeeping is not your tax preparer.

Your bookkeeper compiles the numbers in categories that you will give to your tax preparer. The tax preparer may serve as your bookkeeper too, but they are indeed two contrasting functions.

You may have a relationship where your preparer would be willing and able to do more for you, but you have failed to initiate more engagement.

The answer to not knowing how well you are being taken care of regarding tax prep is to take your data to an impartial professional outside of the firm that you are using.

You engage this new set of eyes and knowledge base for an in-depth review and discussion to see if there are areas that could be improved or discussed with your current preparer to maintain the relationship.

People ask for a second or third opinion all the time on medical issues. Why don't you ask for a second opinion on tax issues? It makes sense to periodically have a second opinion on your tax returns for a tax bill that you will pay thousands and thousands of dollars for each year.

Do you agree?

Have you ever sought out a second or third opinion on your taxes?

Why or why not?

In the next chapter we will go over an example of how I review records for a potential new client in my practice acting as an initiative-taking tax planner mentioned above.

MONEY WITH AMY SERIES

SELF-EMPLOYED TAXES:
Unleashing Schedule C Deductions

Let me affirm that no tax preparer or tax practice is perfect.

There are hundreds of pages of new tax rules and regulations updated each year.

The majority try to do their best.

Dedicated tax professionals expend more effort than others to stay up to date.

Those who do not want to be initiative taking professionals do not learn anything new year to year and those are the ones I find cost you the most money.

A red flag I see is when you look at the bottom of the 1040 form page two when flushing out professionals and those who are not professionals. Did the person you paid to prepare your return sign and take credit for doing it? If you paid a person to do your taxes and is says "Self-Prepared" you are on your own. They do not want to be found or accountable for what they put on the pages.

Paid Preparer Use Only	Preparer's name	Preparer's signature	Date	PTIN	Check if. Self-employed
	Firm's name			Phone no.	
	Firm's address			Firm's EIN	

Go to www.irs.gov/Form1040 for instructions and the latest information.   Form **1040** (2022)

How do you know if they are trying to keep up? Easy! Ask any preparer about the number of Continuing Education (CE) hours they completed last year. If they say "zero," there is your answer, they are no longer trying to keep up to date. I am required at this writing to do at least 18 hours CE annually, and easily will do double that minimum requirement.

If they say X, hours a good easy follow-up question would be "What designations do you maintain?" If they do not have any designations, why?

Yes, if you are wondering, I do substantial CE hours every year to maintain my designations. That is what real, accountable professionals do!

In the insert above, on your tax return where you paid someone to prepare them for you, are the boxes completed with the PTIN number and Firm's EIN number filled in? If not, that is another red flag they do not want to be associated with preparing your return for some reason.

If you were inquiring about being my client, regardless of your geographic location, we would start here as a reference point:

Step #1

You will provide the last three years of tax returns, all pages, to go over in an in person or Zoom meeting at a time we have agreed upon.

I usually recommend that a client set aside 90 minutes to two hours for this appointment.

I have completed these appointments in less than an hour in other cases.

In other cases, upon review of the returns, we realize that there is a recurring issue, error or missed tax savings opportunity and the discussion takes longer because of the discovery.

Step #2

Using a fresh set of eyes, I will ask you questions about the entries on the forms year by year.

This is a conversation-based meeting using the tax returns filed as our reference point.

I may be looking for mistakes, missed carryover credits, missed deduction entries, your business patterns, and any missed opportunities to rearrange items on the return to your tax advantage.

Step #3

If errors are found that could or should be corrected with amended returns, we calculate the potential refunds to see if it is worth the time to gather the missing deduction backup records to submit amended returns or learn from the past and not repeat the mistake going forward.

In cases where filing amended returns is warranted, we can only file amended returns for the prior three filed tax years. There are limited exceptions to this three-year deadline limit.

You forfeit any refunds over three years old.

Time is the enemy here.

Step #4

I create a written list of items to modify or add to your recordkeeping to incorporate tax saving changes by the end of the current tax year.

Step #5

I have created a written list of items to modify or add to your recordkeeping to incorporate tax saving changes to start at the beginning of the next tax year.

Step #6

We may do a current year tax projection and change a W4 form if you have W2 wages or your quarterly estimates to remit through the remainder of the current tax year.

It is important to understand that when we hold this meeting to do a projection for the current tax year, many months have already passed. We are playing catch up whether we owe more in taxes, or we will owe less. We will adjust tax remittances for the remaining months of the current tax year.

Depending on when a meeting like this would take place, you may have only three months left in the tax year, or six, it all depends on when you would hold the meeting throughout the tax year.

I frequently do a new preliminary tax projection for the coming tax year to enable taxpayers to adjust withholding allowances or quarterly estimates once again when they have an entire tax year to work with. In addition, when you have the actual tax years prepared for the prior year you can adjust this again if necessary.

Step #7

We repeat this process at least annually as circumstances and tax laws change.

Can you do this process with another tax professional?

Of course, you can, but they may not run their practice the way I run mine in this area.

Ask how they manage reviews of returns filed in the recent past, current preparation and future tax projections in their practice.

Not all tax practices are built the same way.

To prepare for our next chapter , please grab three different colored highlighters and print off your 2022 tax return, or the most recent one you have filed. We will discuss entries on the 1040 form and all other forms as we move through the chapters.

MONEY WITH AMY SERIES

SELF-EMPLOYED TAXES:
Unleashing Schedule C Deductions

I know you are ready to jump right in and start learning how to pay less in taxes.

Before we can do that, I need you to understand how Federal tax brackets work.

Why?

It will be much more meaningful to you to see what type of tax savings potential you may have when it comes to a process I call "working the brackets" on each new tax break you learn about in this book.

It will not matter what tax bracket you are in right now to get started.

Once you understand the concept of "working the brackets" it is a lifelong advantage no matter how often Congress changes tax rates.

From all the discussions I have in my sessions with the public in my educational sessions, and one on one meetings with entrepreneurs, no one is having this in-depth conversation with you.

I am delighted you are here now to learn these secrets to help you retain wealth and pass these concepts on to your families.

To frame the discussion for this point before we start working at whittling your tax liability down, I would like you to take a minute to get your 2022 taxes for reference.

It will help you to look at your most recent tax return starting on the 1040 Page 1.

If you are holding a 2022 return in your hand you will refer to line 15 that says, "taxable income."

You may want to pull out the last three years of filed returns to see how that taxable income number has changed over the last few years.

This is the number we will use to determine what your tax bracket will be on what we will refer to as your last dollars in the door for taxation purposes.

These are also the first dollars removed from your return when we increase deductions.

Because state income taxes can vary from 0% in states that do not impose income taxes, and they go up from there. We will not be discussing those at this time to keep it simple.

The concepts on State Income Taxes you will learn here are compatible with the concepts of Federal income tax reduction. Whenever your Federal taxable income drops, so will your taxable state income. The two taxing bodies hold hands!

Reducing your self-employment earnings changes the duo above into a trio of taxing bodies holding hands with the Federal and State taxes when you reduce your taxable self-employment earnings subject to Medicare and FICA taxes.

Reducing taxable income for self-employed individuals has a tax reducing domino effect!

Here are the 2022 tax bracket charts we will use for reference on chapter discussions. Note that in this case the Single and Married Filing Separately Federal income Tax rates are the same until they diverge at the 35% taxation level. I found these charts on the IRS website at: https://www.irs.com/en/2022-federal-income-tax-brackets-rates-standard-deductions/

Single/Unmarried Individuals

Taxable Income	Tax Rate
$0 – $10,275	10%
$10,276 – $41,775	$1,027.50 + 12% of the amount over $10,275
$41,776 – $89,075	$4,807.50 + 22% of the amount over $41,775
$89,076 – $170,050	$15,213.50 + 24% of the amount over $89,075
$170,051 – $215,950	$34,647.50 + 32% of the amount over $170,050
$215,951 – $539,900	$49,335.50 + 35% of the amount over $215,950
$539,901 or more	$162,718 + 37% of the amount over $539,900

Married Filing Jointly or Qualifying Widow/Widower

Taxable Income	Tax Rate
$0 – $20,550	10%
$20,551 – $83,550	$2,055 + 12% of the amount over $20,550
$83,551 – $178,150	$9,615 + 22% of the amount over $83,550
$178,151 – $340,100	$30,427 + 24% of the amount over $178,150
$340,101 – $431,900	$69,295 + 32% of the amount over $340,100
$431,901 – $647,850	$98,671 + 35% of the amount over $431,900
$647,851 or more	$174,253.50 + 37% of the amount over $647,850

Married Filing Separately

Taxable Income	Tax Rate
$0 – $10,275	10%
$10,276 – $41,775	$1,027.50 + 12% of the amount over $10,275
$41,776 – $89,075	$4,807.50 + 22% of the amount over $41,775
$89,076 – $170,050	$15,213.50 + 24% of the amount over $89,075
$170,051 – $215,950	$34,647.50 + 32% of the amount over $170,050
$215,951 – $323,925	$49,335.50 + 35% of the amount over $215,950
$323,926 or more	$86,127 + 37% of the amount over $323,925

Head of Household

Taxable Income	Tax Rate
$0 – $14,650	10%
$14,651 – $55,900	$1,465 + 12% of the amount over $14,650
$55,901 – $89,0505	$6,415 + 22% of the amount over $55,900
$89,051 – $170,050	$13,708 + 24% of the amount over $89,050
$170,051 – $215,950	$33,148.50 + 32% of the amount over $170,050
$215,951 – $539,900	$47,836.50 + 35% of the amount over $215,950
$539,901 or more	$162,218.50 + 37% of the amount over $539,900

In the next chapter we discover how tax brackets work for entrepreneurs who file in the Single tax status.

CHAPTER 4

Example of a Single Entrepreneur with $94,572 in taxable income.

MONEY WITH AMY SERIES

SELF-EMPLOYED TAXES:
Unleashing Schedule C Deductions

This is the sample page 1 of the return we will use for this discussion.

Form 1040 Department of the Treasury—Internal Revenue Service
U.S. Individual Income Tax Return 2022 OMB No. 1545-0074 IRS Use Only—Do not write or staple in this space.

Filing Status
Check only one box.
[X] Single [ ] Married filing jointly [ ] Married filing separately (MFS) [ ] Head of household (HOH) [ ] Qualifying surviving spouse (QSS)

If you checked the MFS box, enter the name of your spouse. If you checked the HOH or QSS box, enter the child's name if the qualifying person is a child but not your dependent.

Your first name and middle initial	Last name	Your social security number
SINGLE	ENTREPRENEUR	012-34-5678
If joint return, spouse's first name and middle initial	Last name	Spouse's social security number

Home address (number and street). If you have a P.O. box, see instructions. 123 OPTIMISTIC LANE   Apt. no.

City, town, or post office. If you have a foreign address, also complete spaces below. TOPEKA   State KS   ZIP code 66611

Foreign country name   Foreign province/state/county   Foreign postal code

Presidential Election Campaign
Check here if you, or your spouse if filing jointly, want $3 to go to this fund. Checking a box below will not change your tax or refund.
[ ] You [ ] Spouse

Digital Assets
At any time during 2022, did you: (a) receive (as a reward, award, or payment for property or services); or (b) sell, exchange, gift, or otherwise dispose of a digital asset (or a financial interest in a digital asset)? (See instructions.) [ ] Yes [X] No

Standard Deduction
Someone can claim: [ ] You as a dependent [ ] Your spouse as a dependent
[ ] Spouse itemizes on a separate return or you were a dual-status alien

Age/Blindness You: [ ] Were born before January 2, 1958 [ ] Are blind   Spouse: [ ] Was born before January 2, 1958 [ ] Is blind

Dependents (see instructions):
If more than four dependents, see instructions and check here [ ]

(1) First name Last name	(2) Social security number	(3) Relationship to you	(4) Check the box if qualifies for (see instructions): Child tax credit	Credit for other dependents
			[ ]	[ ]
			[ ]	[ ]
			[ ]	[ ]
			[ ]	[ ]

Income
Attach Form(s) W-2 here. Also attach Forms W-2G and 1099-R if tax was withheld.
If you did not get a Form W-2, see instructions.
Attach Sch. B if required.

1a	Total amount from Form(s) W-2, box 1 (see instructions)	1a	
b	Household employee wages not reported on Form(s) W-2	1b	
c	Tip income not reported on line 1a (see instructions)	1c	
d	Medicaid waiver payments not reported on Form(s) W-2 (see instructions)	1d	
e	Taxable dependent care benefits from Form 2441, line 26	1e	
f	Employer-provided adoption benefits from Form 8839, line 29	1f	
g	Wages from Form 8919, line 6	1g	
h	Other earned income (see instructions)	1h	
i	Nontaxable combat pay election (see instructions) 1i		
z	Add lines 1a through 1h	1z	
2a	Tax-exempt interest 2a	b Taxable interest	2b 0.
3a	Qualified dividends 3a	b Ordinary dividends	3b 0.
4a	IRA distributions 4a	b Taxable amount	4b
5a	Pensions and annuities 5a	b Taxable amount	5b
6a	Social security benefits 6a	b Taxable amount	6b
c	If you elect to use the lump-sum election method, check here (see instructions) [ ]		
7	Capital gain or (loss). Attach Schedule D if required. If not required, check here [ ]	7	
8	Other income from Schedule 1, line 10	8	141,136.
9	Add lines 1z, 2b, 3b, 4b, 5b, 6b, 7, and 8. This is your **total income**	9	141,136.
10	Adjustments to income from Schedule 1, line 26	10	9,971.
11	Subtract line 10 from line 9. This is your **adjusted gross income**	11	131,165.
12	Standard deduction or itemized deductions (from Schedule A)	12	12,950.
13	Qualified business income deduction from Form 8995 or Form 8995-A	13	23,643.
14	Add lines 12 and 13	14	36,593.
15	Subtract line 14 from line 11. If zero or less, enter -0-. This is your **taxable income**	15	94,572.

Standard Deduction for—
• Single or Married filing separately, $12,950
• Married filing jointly or Qualifying surviving spouse, $25,900
• Head of household, $19,400
• If you checked any box under Standard Deduction, see instructions.

For Disclosure, Privacy Act, and Paperwork Reduction Act Notice, see separate instructions.   Form **1040** (2022)

14

Tax and Credits	16	Tax (see instructions). Check if any from Form(s): 1 ☐ 8814 2 ☐ 4972 3 ☐ _____		16	16,534.
	17	Amount from Schedule 2, line 3		17	
	18	Add lines 16 and 17		18	16,534.
	19	Child tax credit or credit for other dependents from Schedule 8812		19	
	20	Amount from Schedule 3, line 8		20	
	21	Add lines 19 and 20		21	
	22	Subtract line 21 from line 18. If zero or less, enter -0-		22	16,534.
	23	Other taxes, including self-employment tax, from Schedule 2, line 21		23	19,942.
	24	Add lines 22 and 23. This is your **total tax**		24	36,476.

Payments	25	Federal income tax withheld from:			
	a	Form(s) W-2	25a		
	b	Form(s) 1099	25b		
	c	Other forms (see instructions)	25c		
	d	Add lines 25a through 25c		25d	
If you have a qualifying child, attach Sch. EIC.	26	2022 estimated tax payments and amount applied from 2021 return		26	
	27	Earned income credit (EIC) . . . . . . No	27		
	28	Additional child tax credit from Schedule 8812	28		
	29	American opportunity credit from Form 8863, line 8	29		
	30	Reserved for future use	30		
	31	Amount from Schedule 3, line 15	31		
	32	Add lines 27, 28, 29, and 31. These are your **total other payments and refundable credits**		32	
	33	Add lines 25d, 26, and 32. These are your **total payments**		33	

Refund	34	If line 33 is more than line 24, subtract line 24 from line 33. This is the amount you **overpaid**		34	
	35a	Amount of line 34 you want **refunded to you.** If Form 8888 is attached, check here ☐		35a	
Direct deposit? See instructions.	b	Routing number X X X X X X X X X c Type: ☐ Checking ☐ Savings			
	d	Account number X X X X X X X X X X X X X X X X X			
	36	Amount of line 34 you want **applied to your 2023 estimated tax**	36		

Amount You Owe	37	Subtract line 33 from line 24. This is the **amount you owe.** For details on how to pay, go to *www.irs.gov/Payments* or see instructions		37	36,476.
	38	Estimated tax penalty (see instructions)	38		

Third Party Designee	Do you want to allow another person to discuss this return with the IRS? See instructions	☐ **Yes.** Complete below. ☒ **No**
	Designee's name	Phone no.	Personal identification number (PIN)

Sign Here

Under penalties of perjury, I declare that I have examined this return and accompanying schedules and statements, and to the best of my knowledge and belief, they are true, correct, and complete. Declaration of preparer (other than taxpayer) is based on all information of which preparer has any knowledge.

	Your signature	Date	Your occupation ENTREPRENEUR	If the IRS sent you an Identity Protection PIN, enter it here (see inst.)
Joint return? See instructions. Keep a copy for your records.	Spouse's signature. If a joint return, **both** must sign.	Date	Spouse's occupation	If the IRS sent your spouse an Identity Protection PIN, enter it here (see inst.)
	Phone no.		Email address	

Paid Preparer Use Only	Preparer's name Amy Rose Herrick	Preparer's signature Amy Rose Herrick	Date 07/27/2023	PTIN P00581983	Check if: ☒ Self-employed
	Firm's name Amy Rose Herrick			Phone no. (785) 224-8954	
	Firm's address 5020 State Solitude Christiansted VI 00820			Firm's EIN 74-2854800	

Go to *www.irs.gov/Form1040* for instructions and the latest information.   **BAA**   REV 07/10/23 PRO   Form **1040** (2022)

2022 tax table: single filers

Tax rate	Taxable income bracket	Tax owed
10%	$0 to $10,275.	10% of taxable income.
12%	$10,276 to $41,775.	$1,027.50 plus 12% of the amount over $10,275.
22%	$41,776 to $89,075.	$4,807.50 plus 22% of the amount over $41,775.
24%	$89,076 to $170,050.	$15,213.50 plus 24% of the amount over $89,075.
32%	$170,051 to $215,950.	$34,647.50 plus 32% of the amount over $170,050.
35%	$215,951 to $539,900.	$49,335.50 plus 35% of the amount over $215,950.
37%	$539,901 or more.	$162,718 plus 37% of the amount over $539,900.

I want to spend a few minutes here because few people understand that tax brackets are progressive based on income, and you are not taxed a flat rate on all your income.

We need an example to work a little math magic.

In this first example, we will pretend that you are the "Single Entrepreneur" on the return inserted above.

On your hypothetical 2022 1040, line 15, the number $94,572 is your Federal taxable income after all deductions have been removed.

Using the chart above the first $10,275 is taxed at 10%.

The amount between $10,276 and $41,775 is taxed at 12%. Most of my clients are not going to notice much of a difference between 10 and 12% taxation.

You will recognize in your tax bill the next step up which is a 22% tax rate.

Now for our example we will also be maxing out the 22% tax bracket on income between $41,776 and $89,075.

You will notice in our example the $94,572 of taxable income puts only $5,497 of income in the 24% tax bracket.

This means the first $5,497 in new deductions that we can identify will save us $0.24 on the dollar in federal income taxes.

Any new deductions over the $5,497 amount will have a $0.22 on the dollar in federal income tax reduction effect.

This is only part of the taxation picture if you are in a location that levies a state income tax. That tax rate would also apply to your tax savings depending on the brackets that may exist in your state using a chart that may look like the one above that is levied on the federal income tax portion.

When you are self-employed using a schedule C you would need to look on the 2022 return on the schedule one line 3 to see what your taxable income is specifically related to the profits in your business after all expenses have been deducted from your gross income.

This number is subject to Social Security taxes which is approximately 15 percent that is remitted to Social Security. If you live in one of the US territories like the US Virgin Islands, you will remit this tax separately and it will not be on your 1040 return.

Circling back to the example $94,5725 taxable income for this "Single Entrepreneur", we can see the last dollars earned would be subject to 24% federal income taxes, 15% in Social Security taxes meaning we expect to lose $0.39 on the dollar to taxation on our profits.

If you live in a state with state income taxes and we will pretend that that is a flat 5%, then on every profit dollar you would need to set aside $0.44 on the dollar for these three taxes levied. OUCH!

If you live in a state that also imposes a gross receipts taxes, that could be another percentage that is lost to taxation for this entrepreneur.

If this taxpayer were able to reduce their taxable income by only $5,000, at the 39% taxation rate that would be a reduction in taxes of $1,950 for only this tax year.

Are you doing anything else that reduces your costs by 39%?

Take my word for it, you will not gain all your tax savings in one area. Usually, it is a combination of several different areas that add up to a substantial difference on your return.

What is the average federal tax rate for this entrepreneur?

When I look at page two of the 1040 return, we see the taxes on the 1040 line 24 gives the amount of Federal taxes due of $36,476.

Tax and Credits					
	16	**Tax** (see instructions). Check if any from Form(s): **1** ☐ 8814 **2** ☐ 4972 **3** ☐ _____		16	16,534.
	17	Amount from Schedule 2, line 3		17	
	18	Add lines 16 and 17		18	16,534.
	19	Child tax credit or credit for other dependents from Schedule 8812		19	
	20	Amount from Schedule 3, line 8		20	
	21	Add lines 19 and 20		21	
	22	Subtract line 21 from line 18. If zero or less, enter -0-		22	16,534.
	23	Other taxes, including self-employment tax, from Schedule 2, line 21		23	19,942.
	24	Add lines 22 and 23. This is your **total tax**		24	36,476.

We take the $36,476 tax divided by the 1040-line 15 taxable income of $94,572 to reach an average tax rate across multiple tax brackets of 38.5%.

In the next chapter we discover how tax brackets work for entrepreneurs who file in the Head of Household tax status.

CHAPTER 5

Example of a Head of Household Entrepreneur with two children under the age of 12 with $122,525 in taxable income.

MONEY WITH AMY SERIES

SELF-EMPLOYED TAXES:
Unleashing Schedule C Deductions

This is the sample page 1 of the return we will use for this discussion

Form 1040 Department of the Treasury—Internal Revenue Service
U.S. Individual Income Tax Return **2022** OMB No. 1545-0074 IRS Use Only—Do not write or staple in this space.

Filing Status
Check only one box.
☐ Single ☐ Married filing jointly ☐ Married filing separately (MFS) ☒ Head of household (HOH) ☐ Qualifying surviving spouse (QSS)

If you checked the MFS box, enter the name of your spouse. If you checked the HOH or QSS box, enter the child's name if the qualifying person is a child but not your dependent.

Your first name and middle initial	Last name	Your social security number
HEAD OF HOUSEHOLD	ENTREPRENEUR	012-34-5678
If joint return, spouse's first name and middle initial	Last name	Spouse's social security number

Home address (number and street). If you have a P.O. box, see instructions.		Apt. no.	Presidential Election Campaign
123 OPTIMISTIC LANE			Check here if you, or your spouse if filing jointly, want $3 to go to this fund. Checking a box below will not change your tax or refund.

City, town, or post office. If you have a foreign address, also complete spaces below.	State	ZIP code	
TOPEKA	KS	66611	☐ You ☐ Spouse

Foreign country name	Foreign province/state/county	Foreign postal code

Digital Assets
At any time during 2022, did you: (a) receive (as a reward, award, or payment for property or services); or (b) sell, exchange, gift, or otherwise dispose of a digital asset (or a financial interest in a digital asset)? (See instructions.) ☐ Yes ☒ No

Standard Deduction
Someone can claim: ☐ You as a dependent ☐ Your spouse as a dependent
☐ Spouse itemizes on a separate return or you were a dual-status alien

Age/Blindness You: ☐ Were born before January 2, 1958 ☐ Are blind **Spouse:** ☐ Was born before January 2, 1958 ☐ Is blind

Dependents (see instructions):
If more than four dependents, see instructions and check here ☐

(1) First name Last name	(2) Social security number	(3) Relationship to you	(4) Check the box if qualifies for (see instructions): Child tax credit	Credit for other dependents
BELLA ENTREPRENEUR	234-56-7890	Daughter	☒	☐
XAVIER ENTREPRENEUR	345-67-8901	Son	☒	☐
			☐	☐
			☐	☐

Income

Attach Form(s) W-2 here. Also attach Forms W-2G and 1099-R if tax was withheld.

If you did not get a Form W-2, see instructions.

1a	Total amount from Form(s) W-2, box 1 (see instructions)	1a	
b	Household employee wages not reported on Form(s) W-2	1b	
c	Tip income not reported on line 1a (see instructions)	1c	
d	Medicaid waiver payments not reported on Form(s) W-2 (see instructions)	1d	
e	Taxable dependent care benefits from Form 2441, line 26	1e	
f	Employer-provided adoption benefits from Form 8839, line 29	1f	
g	Wages from Form 8919, line 6	1g	
h	Other earned income (see instructions)	1h	
i	Nontaxable combat pay election (see instructions) 1i		
z	Add lines 1a through 1h	1z	

Attach Sch. B if required.

2a	Tax-exempt interest	2a		b Taxable interest	2b	0.
3a	Qualified dividends	3a		b Ordinary dividends	3b	0.
4a	IRA distributions	4a		b Taxable amount	4b	
5a	Pensions and annuities	5a		b Taxable amount	5b	
6a	Social security benefits	6a		b Taxable amount	6b	
c	If you elect to use the lump-sum election method, check here (see instructions) ☐					
7	Capital gain or (loss). Attach Schedule D if required. If not required, check here ☐				7	

Standard Deduction for—
- Single or Married filing separately, $12,950
- Married filing jointly or Qualifying surviving spouse, $25,900
- Head of household, $19,400
- If you checked any box under Standard Deduction, see instructions.

8	Other income from Schedule 1, line 10	8	184,136.
9	Add lines 1z, 2b, 3b, 4b, 5b, 6b, 7, and 8. This is your **total income**	9	184,136.
10	Adjustments to income from Schedule 1, line 26	10	11,580.
11	Subtract line 10 from line 9. This is your **adjusted gross income**	11	172,556.
12	Standard deduction or itemized deductions (from Schedule A)	12	19,400.
13	Qualified business income deduction from Form 8995 or Form 8995-A	13	30,631.
14	Add lines 12 and 13	14	50,031.
15	Subtract line 14 from line 11. If zero or less, enter -0-. This is your **taxable income**	15	122,525.

For Disclosure, Privacy Act, and Paperwork Reduction Act Notice, see separate instructions. Form **1040** (2022)

20

Tax and Credits	16	**Tax** (see instructions). Check if any from Form(s): **1** ☐ 8814 **2** ☐ 4972 **3** ☐ _____		16	21,742.
	17	Amount from Schedule 2, line 3		17	
	18	Add lines 16 and 17		18	21,742.
	19	Child tax credit or credit for other dependents from Schedule 8812		19	4,000.
	20	Amount from Schedule 3, line 8		20	
	21	Add lines 19 and 20		21	4,000.
	22	Subtract line 21 from line 18. If zero or less, enter -0-		22	17,742.
	23	Other taxes, including self-employment tax, from Schedule 2, line 21		23	23,159.
	24	Add lines 22 and 23. This is your **total tax**		24	40,901.
Payments	25	Federal income tax withheld from:			
	a	Form(s) W-2	25a		
	b	Form(s) 1099	25b		
	c	Other forms (see instructions)	25c		
	d	Add lines 25a through 25c		25d	
If you have a qualifying child, attach Sch. EIC.	26	2022 estimated tax payments and amount applied from 2021 return		26	
	27	Earned income credit (EIC) . . . . No.	27		
	28	Additional child tax credit from Schedule 8812	28		
	29	American opportunity credit from Form 8863, line 8	29		
	30	Reserved for future use	30		
	31	Amount from Schedule 3, line 15	31		
	32	Add lines 27, 28, 29, and 31. These are your **total other payments and refundable credits**		32	
	33	Add lines 25d, 26, and 32. These are your **total payments**		33	
Refund	34	If line 33 is more than line 24, subtract line 24 from line 33. This is the amount you **overpaid**		34	
	35a	Amount of line 34 you want **refunded to you**. If Form 8888 is attached, check here ☐		35a	
Direct deposit? See instructions.	b	Routing number X|X|X|X|X|X|X|X|X| **c** Type: ☐ Checking ☐ Savings			
	d	Account number X|X|X|X|X|X|X|X|X|X|X|X|X|X|X|X|X			
	36	Amount of line 34 you want **applied to your 2023 estimated tax**	36		
Amount You Owe	37	Subtract line 33 from line 24. This is the **amount you owe.** For details on how to pay, go to *www.irs.gov/Payments* or see instructions		37	40,901.
	38	Estimated tax penalty (see instructions)	38		

Third Party Designee

Do you want to allow another person to discuss this return with the IRS? See instructions . . . . ☐ **Yes.** Complete below. ☒ **No**

Designee's name	Phone no.	Personal identification number (PIN)				

Sign Here

Under penalties of perjury, I declare that I have examined this return and accompanying schedules and statements, and to the best of my knowledge and belief, they are true, correct, and complete. Declaration of preparer (other than taxpayer) is based on all information of which preparer has any knowledge.

Your signature	Date	Your occupation ENTREPRENEUR	If the IRS sent you an Identity Protection PIN, enter it here (see inst.)
Joint return? See instructions. Keep a copy for your records. Spouse's signature. If a joint return, **both** must sign.	Date	Spouse's occupation	If the IRS sent your spouse an Identity Protection PIN, enter it here (see inst.)
Phone no.	Email address		

Paid Preparer Use Only

Preparer's name	Preparer's signature	Date	PTIN	Check if:
Amy Rose Herrick	Amy Rose Herrick	07/27/2023	P00581983	☒ Self-employed
Firm's name Amy Rose Herrick			Phone no.	(785)224-8954
Firm's address 5020 State Solitude Christiansted VI 00820			Firm's EIN	74-2854800

Go to *www.irs.gov/Form1040* for instructions and the latest information.   **BAA**   REV 07/10/23 PRO   Form **1040** (2022)

2022 tax table: head of household

Tax rate	Taxable income bracket	Tax owed
10%	$0 to $14,650.	10% of taxable income.
12%	$14,651 to $55,900.	$1,465 plus 12% of the amount over $14,650.
22%	$55,901 to $89,050.	$6,415 plus 22% of the amount over $55,900.
24%	$89,051 to $170,050.	$13,708 plus 24% of the amount over $89,050.
32%	$170,051 to $215,950.	$33,148 plus 32% of the amount over $170,050.
35%	$215,951 to $539,900.	$47,836 plus 35% of the amount over $215,950.
37%	$539,901 or more.	$161,218.50 plus 37% of the amount over $539,900.

In this example, we will pretend that you are the "Head of Household Entrepreneur" on the return inserted above.

On your hypothetical 2022 1040, line 15, the number $122,525 is your Federal taxable income after all deductions have been removed.

Using the chart above the first $14,650 is taxed at 10%.

The amount between $14,651 and $55,900 is taxed at 12%. Most of my clients are not going to notice much of a difference between 10 and 12% taxation.

You will recognize in your tax bill the next step up which is a 22% tax rate.

Now for our example we will also be maxing out the 22% tax bracket on income between $55,900 and $89,050.

You will notice in our example the $122,525 of taxable income puts $33,475 of income in the 24% tax bracket.

This means the first $33,475 in new deductions that we can identify will save us $0.24 on the dollar in federal income taxes.

Any new deductions over the $33,475 amount will have a $0.22 on the dollar in federal income tax reduction effect.

This is only part of the taxation picture if you are in a location that levies a state income tax. That tax rate would also apply to your tax savings depending on the brackets that may exist in your state using a chart that may look like the one above that is levied on the federal income tax portion.

When you are self-employed using a schedule C you would need to look on the 2022 return on the schedule one line 3 to see what your taxable income is specifically related to the profits in your business after all expenses have been deducted from your gross income.

But wait, we have a new tax twist here behind the scenes.

Self-Employment Tax

Go to *www.irs.gov/ScheduleSE* for instructions and the latest information.

Attach to Form 1040, 1040-SR, or 1040-NR.

OMB No. 1545-0074

2022

Attachment
Sequence No. **17**

Name of person with self-employment income (as shown on Form 1040, 1040-SR, or 1040-NR)	Social security number of person with **self-employment** income
HEAD OF HOUSEHOLD ENTREPRENEUR	012-34-5678

Part I   Self-Employment Tax

Note: If your only income subject to self-employment tax is **church employee income**, see instructions for how to report your income and the definition of church employee income.

A   If you are a minister, member of a religious order, or Christian Science practitioner **and** you filed Form 4361, but you had $400 or more of **other** net earnings from self-employment, check here and continue with Part I   ☐

Skip lines 1a and 1b if you use the farm optional method in Part II. See instructions.

1a	Net farm profit or (loss) from Schedule F, line 34, and farm partnerships, Schedule K-1 (Form 1065), box 14, code A	**1a**	
b	If you received social security retirement or disability benefits, enter the amount of Conservation Reserve Program payments included on Schedule F, line 4b, or listed on Schedule K-1 (Form 1065), box 20, code AH	**1b**	( )

Skip line 2 if you use the nonfarm optional method in Part II. See instructions.

2	Net profit or (loss) from Schedule C, line 31; and Schedule K-1 (Form 1065), box 14, code A (other than farming). See instructions for other income to report or if you are a minister or member of a religious order	**2**	184,136.
3	Combine lines 1a, 1b, and 2	**3**	184,136.
4a	If line 3 is more than zero, multiply line 3 by 92.35% (0.9235). Otherwise, enter amount from line 3	**4a**	170,050.
	Note: If line 4a is less than $400 due to Conservation Reserve Program payments on line 1b, see instructions.		
b	If you elect one or both of the optional methods, enter the total of lines 15 and 17 here	**4b**	
c	Combine lines 4a and 4b. If less than $400, **stop**, you don't owe self-employment tax. **Exception:** If less than $400 and you had **church employee income**, enter -0- and continue	**4c**	170,050.
5a	Enter your **church employee income** from Form W-2. See instructions for definition of church employee income	**5a**	
b	Multiply line 5a by 92.35% (0.9235). If less than $100, enter -0-	**5b**	0.
6	Add lines 4c and 5b	**6**	170,050.
7	Maximum amount of combined wages and self-employment earnings subject to social security tax or the 6.2% portion of the 7.65% railroad retirement (tier 1) tax for 2022	**7**	147,000
8a	Total social security wages and tips (total of boxes 3 and 7 on Form(s) W-2) and railroad retirement (tier 1) compensation. If $147,000 or more, skip lines 8b through 10, and go to line 11	**8a**	
b	Unreported tips subject to social security tax from Form 4137, line 10	**8b**	
c	Wages subject to social security tax from Form 8919, line 10	**8c**	
d	Add lines 8a, 8b, and 8c	**8d**	
9	Subtract line 8d from line 7. If zero or less, enter -0- here and on line 10 and go to line 11	**9**	147,000.
10	Multiply the **smaller** of line 6 or line 9 by 12.4% (0.124)	**10**	18,228.
11	Multiply line 6 by 2.9% (0.029)	**11**	4,931.
12	**Self-employment tax.** Add lines 10 and 11. Enter here and on **Schedule 2 (Form 1040), line 4**	**12**	23,159.
13	**Deduction for one-half of self-employment tax.** Multiply line 12 by 50% (0.50). Enter here and on **Schedule 1 (Form 1040), line 15**	**13**	11,580.

Part II   Optional Methods To Figure Net Earnings (see instructions)

Farm Optional Method. You may use this method **only** if **(a)** your gross farm income[1] wasn't more than $9,060, **or (b)** your net farm profits[3] were less than $6,540.

14	Maximum income for optional methods	**14**	6,040
15	Enter the **smaller** of: two-thirds (⅔) of gross farm income[1] (not less than zero) or $6,040. Also, include this amount on line 4b above	**15**	

Nonfarm Optional Method. You may use this method **only** if **(a)** your net nonfarm profits[3] were less than $6,540 and also less than 72.189% of your gross nonfarm income,[4] **and (b)** you had net earnings from self-employment of at least $400 in 2 of the prior 3 years. **Caution:** You may use this method no more than five times.

16	Subtract line 15 from line 14	**16**	
17	Enter the **smaller** of: two-thirds (⅔) of gross nonfarm income[4] (not less than zero) **or** the amount on line 16. Also, include this amount on line 4b above	**17**	

[1] From Sch. F, line 9; and Sch. K-1 (Form 1065), box 14, code B.
[3] From Sch. F, line 34; and Sch. K-1 (Form 1065), box 14, code A—minus the amount you would have entered on line 1b had you not used the optional method.
[2] From Sch. C, line 31; and Sch. K-1 (Form 1065), box 14, code A.
[4] From Sch. C, line 7; and Sch. K-1 (Form 1065), box 14, code C.

For Paperwork Reduction Act Notice, see your tax return instructions.   BAA   REV 07/10/23 PRO   Schedule SE (Form 1040) 2022

This entrepreneur exceeded the $147,000 threshold for the Social Security tax levies to be imposed at 12.4% on self-employment. That means any taxable self-employment over $147,000 would not be subject to a 12.4% tax calculation.

However, all self-employment earnings with no ceiling are subject to the 2.9% Medicare levy.

Circling back to the example $122,525 taxable income for this "Head of Household Entrepreneur", we can see the last dollars earned would be subject to 24% federal income taxes, 2.9 % in Social Security taxes meaning we expect to lose $0.269 on the last dollars to taxation on our profits.

If you live in a state with state income taxes and we will pretend that that is a flat 5%, then on every profit dollar you would need to set aside $0.319 on the dollar for these three taxes levied. OUCH!

If you live in a state that also imposes a gross receipts taxes, that could be another percentage that is lost to taxation for this entrepreneur.

If this taxpayer were able to reduce their taxable income by only $10,000, at the .319% taxation rate that would be a reduction in taxes of $3,190 for only this tax year.

Are you doing anything else that reduces your costs by 31.9%?

Take my word for it, you will not gain all your tax savings in one area. Usually, it is a combination of several different areas that add up to a substantial difference on your return.

What is the average federal tax rate for this entrepreneur?

When I look at page two of the 1040return we see the taxes on the 1040 line 24 gives the amount of Federal taxes due of $40,901 after the child tax credits are applied.

Form 1040 (2022)				Page 2
Tax and	16	Tax (see instructions). Check if any from Form(s). 1 ☐ 8814 2 ☐ 4972 3 ☐ ____	16	21,742.
Credits	17	Amount from Schedule 2, line 3	17	
	18	Add lines 16 and 17	18	21,742.
	19	Child tax credit or credit for other dependents from Schedule 8812	19	4,000.
	20	Amount from Schedule 3, line 8	20	
	21	Add lines 19 and 20	21	4,000.
	22	Subtract line 21 from line 18. If zero or less, enter -0-	22	17,742.
	23	Other taxes, including self-employment tax, from Schedule 2, line 21	23	23,159.
	24	Add lines 22 and 23. This is your **total tax**	24	40,901.

We take the $40,901 tax divided by the 1040-line 15 Adjusted Gross income of $122,525 to reach an average tax rate across multiple tax brackets of 33.3%.

In the next chapter we discover how tax brackets work for entrepreneurs who file in the Married filing jointly tax status.

CHAPTER 6

Example of a Married Entrepreneur, no children with $200,990 in taxable income.

MONEY WITH AMY SERIES

SELF-EMPLOYED TAXES:
Unleashing Schedule C Deductions

Form 1040

Department of the Treasury - Internal Revenue Service

U.S. Individual Income Tax Return

2022

OMB No. 1545-0074 | IRS Use Only - Do not write or staple in this space.

Filing Status
Check only one box.

☐ Single ☒ Married filing jointly ☐ Married filing separately (MFS) ☐ Head of household (HOH) ☐ Qualifying surviving spouse (QSS)

If you checked the MFS box, enter the name of your spouse. If you checked the HOH or QSS box, enter the child's name if the qualifying person is a child but not your dependent.

Your first name and middle initial	Last name	Your social security number
MARRIED FILING JT	ENTREPRENEUR	012-34-5678

If joint return, spouse's first name and middle initial	Last name	Spouse's social security number
SPOUSE	ENTREPRENEUR	789-01-2345

Home address (number and street). If you have a P.O. box, see instructions. — 123 OPTIMISTIC LANE | Apt. no.

City, town, or post office. If you have a foreign address, also complete spaces below. — TOPEKA | State: KS | ZIP code: 66611

Foreign country name | Foreign province/state/county | Foreign postal code

Presidential Election Campaign
Check here if you, or your spouse if filing jointly, want $3 to go to this fund. Checking a box below will not change your tax or refund.   ☐ You ☐ Spouse

Digital Assets
At any time during 2022, did you: (a) receive (as a reward, award, or payment for property or services); or (b) sell, exchange, gift, or otherwise dispose of a digital asset (or a financial interest in a digital asset)? (See instructions.) ☐ Yes ☒ No

Standard Deduction
Someone can claim: ☐ You as a dependent ☐ Your spouse as a dependent
☐ Spouse itemizes on a separate return or you were a dual-status alien

Age/Blindness You: ☐ Were born before January 2, 1958 ☐ Are blind **Spouse:** ☐ Was born before January 2, 1958 ☐ Is blind

Dependents (see instructions):
If more than four dependents, see instructions and check here ☐

(1) First name Last name	(2) Social security number	(3) Relationship to you	(4) Check the box if qualifies for (see instructions): Child tax credit	Credit for other dependents
			☐	☐
			☐	☐
			☐	☐
			☐	☐

Income

Attach Form(s) W-2 here. Also attach Forms W-2G and 1099-R if tax was withheld.

If you did not get a Form W-2, see instructions.

1a	Total amount from Form(s) W-2, box 1 (see instructions)	1a	
b	Household employee wages not reported on Form(s) W-2	1b	
c	Tip income not reported on line 1a (see instructions)	1c	
d	Medicaid waiver payments not reported on Form(s) W-2 (see instructions)	1d	
e	Taxable dependent care benefits from Form 2441, line 26	1e	
f	Employer-provided adoption benefits from Form 8839, line 29	1f	
g	Wages from Form 8919, line 6	1g	
h	Other earned income (see instructions)	1h	
i	Nontaxable combat pay election (see instructions) 1i		
z	Add lines 1a through 1h	1z	

Attach Sch. B if required.

2a	Tax-exempt interest	2a		b Taxable interest	2b	0.
3a	Qualified dividends	3a		b Ordinary dividends	3b	0.
4a	IRA distributions	4a		b Taxable amount	4b	
5a	Pensions and annuities	5a		b Taxable amount	5b	
6a	Social security benefits	6a		b Taxable amount	6b	

Standard Deduction for—
* Single or Married filing separately, $12,950
* Married filing jointly or Qualifying surviving spouse, $25,900
* Head of household, $19,400
* If you checked any box under Standard Deduction, see instructions.

c	If you elect to use the lump-sum election method, check here (see instructions) ☐		
7	Capital gain or (loss). Attach Schedule D if required. If not required, check here ☐	7	
8	Other income from Schedule 1, line 10	8	290,136.
9	Add lines 1z, 2b, 3b, 4b, 5b, 6b, 7, and 8. This is your **total income**	9	290,136.
10	Adjustments to income from Schedule 1, line 26	10	12,999.
11	Subtract line 10 from line 9. This is your **adjusted gross income**	11	277,137.
12	Standard deduction or itemized deductions (from Schedule A)	12	25,900.
13	Qualified business income deduction from Form 8995 or Form 8995-A	13	50,247.
14	Add lines 12 and 13	14	76,147.
15	Subtract line 14 from line 11. If zero or less, enter -0-. This is your **taxable income**	15	200,990.

For Disclosure, Privacy Act, and Paperwork Reduction Act Notice, see separate instructions.

Form **1040** (2022)

28

Tax and Credits	16	**Tax** (see instructions). Check if any from Form(s): **1** ☐ 8814 **2** ☐ 4972 **3** ☐ _____		16	35,909.
	17	Amount from Schedule 2, line 3		17	
	18	Add lines 16 and 17		18	35,909.
	19	Child tax credit or credit for other dependents from Schedule 8812		19	
	20	Amount from Schedule 3, line 8		20	
	21	Add lines 19 and 20		21	
	22	Subtract line 21 from line 18. If zero or less, enter -0-		22	35,909.
	23	Other taxes, including self-employment tax, from Schedule 2, line 21		23	26,159.
	24	Add lines 22 and 23. This is your **total tax**		24	62,068.
Payments	25	Federal income tax withheld from:			
	a	Form(s) W-2	25a		
	b	Form(s) 1099	25b		
	c	Other forms (see instructions)	25c		
	d	Add lines 25a through 25c		25d	
If you have a qualifying child, attach Sch. EIC.	26	2022 estimated tax payments and amount applied from 2021 return		26	
	27	Earned income credit (EIC) .... No.	27		
	28	Additional child tax credit from Schedule 8812	28		
	29	American opportunity credit from Form 8863, line 8	29		
	30	Reserved for future use	30		
	31	Amount from Schedule 3, line 15	31		
	32	Add lines 27, 28, 29, and 31. These are your **total other payments and refundable credits**		32	
	33	Add lines 25d, 26, and 32. These are your **total payments**		33	
Refund	34	If line 33 is more than line 24, subtract line 24 from line 33. This is the amount you **overpaid**		34	
	35a	Amount of line 34 you want **refunded to you**. If Form 8888 is attached, check here ☐		35a	
Direct deposit? See instructions.	b	Routing number X X X X X X X X X **c** Type: ☐ Checking ☐ Savings			
	d	Account number X X X X X X X X X X X X X X X X X			
	36	Amount of line 34 you want **applied to your 2023 estimated tax**	36		
Amount You Owe	37	Subtract line 33 from line 24. This is the **amount you owe**. For details on how to pay, go to *www.irs.gov/Payments* or see instructions		37	62,068.
	38	Estimated tax penalty (see instructions)	38		

Third Party Designee

Do you want to allow another person to discuss this return with the IRS? See instructions .... ☐ **Yes.** Complete below. ☒ **No**

Designee's name	Phone no.	Personal identification number (PIN) ☐☐☐☐☐

Sign Here

Under penalties of perjury, I declare that I have examined this return and accompanying schedules and statements, and to the best of my knowledge and belief, they are true, correct, and complete. Declaration of preparer (other than taxpayer) is based on all information of which preparer has any knowledge.

Joint return? See instructions. Keep a copy for your records.

Your signature	Date	Your occupation	If the IRS sent you an Identity Protection PIN, enter it here (see inst.)
		ENTREPRENEUR	
Spouse's signature. If a joint return, **both** must sign.	Date	Spouse's occupation	If the IRS sent your spouse an Identity Protection PIN, enter it here (see inst.)
		AWESOME PARTNER	
Phone no.		Email address	

Paid Preparer Use Only	Preparer's name	Preparer's signature	Date	PTIN	Check if:
	Amy Rose Herrick	Amy Rose Herrick	07/27/2023	P00581983	☒ Self-employed
	Firm's name Amy Rose Herrick			Phone no. (785) 224-8954	
	Firm's address 5020 State Solitude Christiansted VI 00820			Firm's EIN 74-2854800	

Go to *www.irs.gov/Form1040* for instructions and the latest information.   BAA   REV 07/10/23 PRO   Form **1040** (2022)

2022 tax table: married, filing jointly

Tax rate	Taxable income bracket	Taxes owed
10%	$0 to $20,550.	10% of taxable income.
12%	$20,551 to $83,550.	$2,055 plus 12% of the amount over $20,550.
22%	$83,551 to $178,150.	$9,615 plus 22% of the amount over $83,550.
24%	$178,151 to $340,100.	$30,427 plus 24% of the amount over $178,150.
32%	$340,101 to $431,900.	$69,295 plus 32% of the amount over $340,100.
35%	$431,901 to $647,850.	$98,671 plus 35% of the amount over $431,900.
37%	$647,851 or more.	$174,253.50 plus 37% of the amount over $647,850.

In this example, we will pretend that you are the "Married Filing Jointly Entrepreneur" on the return inserted above.

On your hypothetical 2022 1040, line 15, the number $200,990 is your Federal taxable income after all deductions have been removed.

Using the chart above the first $20,550 is taxed at 10%.

The amount between $20,551 and $83,550 is taxed at 12%. Most of my clients are not going to notice much of a difference between 10 and 12% taxation.

You will recognize in your tax bill the next step up which is a 22% tax rate.

Now for our example we will also be maxing out the 22% tax bracket on income between $83,551 and $178,150.

You will notice in our example the $200,990 of taxable income puts $22,840 of income in the 24% tax bracket.

This means the first $22,840 in new deductions that we can identify will save us $0.24 on the dollar in federal income taxes.

Any new deductions over the $22,840 amount will have a $0.22 on the dollar in federal income tax reduction effect.

This is only part of the taxation picture if you are in a location that levies a state income tax. That tax rate would also apply to your tax savings depending on the brackets that may exist in your state using a chart that may look like the one above that is levied on the federal income tax portion.

When you are self-employed using a schedule C you would need to look on the 2022 return on the schedule one line 3 to see what your taxable income is specifically related to the profits in your business after all expenses have been deducted from your gross income.

But wait, we have a tax twist here behind the scenes.

SCHEDULE SE
(Form 1040)

Department of the Treasury
Internal Revenue Service

Self-Employment Tax

Go to *www.irs.gov/ScheduleSE* for instructions and the latest information.

Attach to Form 1040, 1040-SR, or 1040-NR.

OMB No. 1545-0074

2022

Attachment
Sequence No. **17**

Name of person with self-employment income (as shown on Form 1040, 1040-SR, or 1040-NR)	Social security number of person with **self-employment** income
MARRIED FILING JT ENTREPRENEUR	012-34-5678

Part I — Self-Employment Tax

Note: If your only income subject to self-employment tax is **church employee income**, see instructions for how to report your income and the definition of church employee income.

A If you are a minister, member of a religious order, or Christian Science practitioner **and** you filed Form 4361, but you had $400 or more of **other** net earnings from self-employment, check here and continue with Part I . . . . . . ☐

Skip lines 1a and 1b if you use the farm optional method in Part II. See instructions.

1a	Net farm profit or (loss) from Schedule F, line 34, and farm partnerships, Schedule K-1 (Form 1065), box 14, code A	**1a**	
b	If you received social security retirement or disability benefits, enter the amount of Conservation Reserve Program payments included on Schedule F, line 4b, or listed on Schedule K-1 (Form 1065), box 20, code AH	**1b**	
	Skip line 2 if you use the nonfarm optional method in Part II. See instructions.		
2	Net profit or (loss) from Schedule C, line 31, and Schedule K-1 (Form 1065), box 14, code A (other than farming). See instructions for other income to report or if you are a minister or member of a religious order	**2**	290,136.
3	Combine lines 1a, 1b, and 2	**3**	290,136.
4a	If line 3 is more than zero, multiply line 3 by 92.35% (0.9235). Otherwise, enter amount from line 3	**4a**	267,941.
	Note: If line 4a is less than $400 due to Conservation Reserve Program payments on line 1b, see instructions.		
b	If you elect one or both of the optional methods, enter the total of lines 15 and 17 here	**4b**	
c	Combine lines 4a and 4b. If less than $400, **stop**, you don't owe self-employment tax. **Exception:** If less than $400 and you had **church employee income**, enter -0- and continue	**4c**	267,941.
5a	Enter your **church employee income** from Form W-2. See instructions for definition of church employee income	5a	
b	Multiply line 5a by 92.35% (0.9235). If less than $100, enter -0-	**5b**	0.
6	Add lines 4c and 5b	**6**	267,941.
7	Maximum amount of combined wages and self-employment earnings subject to social security tax or the 6.2% portion of the 7.65% railroad retirement (tier 1) tax for 2022	**7**	147000
8a	Total social security wages and tips (total of boxes 3 and 7 on Form(s) W-2) and railroad retirement (tier 1) compensation. If $147,000 or more, skip lines 8b through 10, and go to line 11	8a	
b	Unreported tips subject to social security tax from Form 4137, line 10	8b	
c	Wages subject to social security tax from Form 8919, line 10	8c	
d	Add lines 8a, 8b, and 8c	**8d**	
9	Subtract line 8d from line 7. If zero or less, enter -0- here and on line 10 and go to line 11	**9**	147,000.
10	Multiply the **smaller** of line 6 or line 9 by 12.4% (0.124)	**10**	18,228.
11	Multiply line 6 by 2.9% (0.029)	**11**	7,770.
12	**Self-employment tax.** Add lines 10 and 11. Enter here and on **Schedule 2 (Form 1040), line 4**	**12**	25,998.
13	**Deduction for one-half of self-employment tax.** Multiply line 12 by 50% (0.50). Enter here and on **Schedule 1 (Form 1040), line 15**	13	12,999.

Part II — Optional Methods To Figure Net Earnings (see instructions)

Farm Optional Method. You may use this method **only** if **(a)** your gross farm income¹ wasn't more than $9,060, **or (b)** your net farm profits² were less than $6,540.

14	Maximum income for optional methods	**14**	6,040
15	Enter the **smaller** of: two-thirds (⅔) of gross farm income¹ (not less than zero) or $6,040. Also, include this amount on line 4b above	**15**	

Nonfarm Optional Method. You may use this method **only** if **(a)** your net nonfarm profits³ were less than $6,540 and also less than 72.189% of your gross nonfarm income,⁴ **and (b)** you had net earnings from self-employment of at least $400 in 2 of the prior 3 years. **Caution:** You may use this method no more than five times.

16	Subtract line 15 from line 14	**16**	
17	Enter the **smaller** of: two-thirds (⅔) of gross nonfarm income⁴ (not less than zero) or the amount on line 16. Also, include this amount on line 4b above	**17**	

¹ From Sch. F, line 9; and Sch. K-1 (Form 1065), box 14, code B.
² From Sch. F, line 34; and Sch. K-1 (Form 1065), box 14, code A — minus the amount you would have entered on line 1b had you not used the optional method.
³ From Sch. C, line 31; and Sch. K-1 (Form 1065), box 14, code A.
⁴ From Sch. C, line 7; and Sch. K-1 (Form 1065), box 14, code C.

For Paperwork Reduction Act Notice, see your tax return instructions. BAA REV 07/19/23 PRO Schedule SE (Form 1040) 2022

This entrepreneur exceeded the $147,000 threshold for the Social Security tax levies to be imposed at 12.4% on self-employment. That means any taxable self-employment over $147,000 would not be subject to a 12.4% tax calculation.

However, all self-employment earnings with no ceiling are subject to the 2.9% Medicare levy.

Circling back to the example $200,990 taxable income for this "Head of Household Entrepreneur", we can see the last dollars earned would be subject to 24% federal income taxes, 2.9 % in Social Security taxes meaning we expect to lose $0.269 on the last dollars to taxation on our profits.

If you live in a state with state income taxes and we will pretend that that is a flat 5%, then on every profit dollar you would need to set aside $0.319 on the dollar for these three taxes levied. OUCH!

If you live in a state that also imposes a gross receipts taxes, that could be another percentage that is lost to taxation for this entrepreneur.

If this taxpayer were able to reduce their taxable income by only $10,000, at the 31.9% taxation rate that would be a reduction in taxes of $3,190 for only this tax year.

Are you doing anything else that reduces your costs by 31.9%?

Take my word for it, you will not gain all your tax savings in one area. Usually, it is a combination of several different areas that add up to a substantial difference on your return.

What is the average federal tax rate for this entrepreneur?

When I look at page two of the 1040return we see the taxes on the 1040 line 24 gives the amount of Federal taxes due of $62,068.

Form 1040 (2022)				Page **2**
Tax and	16	Tax (see instructions). Check if any from Form(s): 1 ☐ 8814 2 ☐ 4972 3 ☐ _____	16	35,909.
Credits	17	Amount from Schedule 2, line 3	17	
	18	Add lines 16 and 17	18	35,909.
	19	Child tax credit or credit for other dependents from Schedule 8812	19	
	20	Amount from Schedule 3, line 8	20	
	21	Add lines 19 and 20	21	
	22	Subtract line 21 from line 18. If zero or less, enter -0-	22	35,909.
	23	Other taxes, including self-employment tax, from Schedule 2, line 21	23	26,159.
	24	Add lines 22 and 23. This is your **total tax**	24	62,068.

We take the $62,068 tax divided by the 1040-line 15 taxable income of $200,990 to reach an average tax rate across multiple tax brackets of 30.8%.

In the next chapter we discover how tax brackets work for entrepreneurs who file in the Married filing separately tax status.

CHAPTER 7

Example of a Married Filing Separately Entrepreneur, one child, with $356,891 in taxable income.

MONEY WITH AMY SERIES

SELF-EMPLOYED TAXES:
Unleashing Schedule C Deductions

Form 1040
U.S. Individual Income Tax Return

Department of the Treasury—Internal Revenue Service

2022 OMB No. 1545-0074 IRS Use Only—Do not write or staple in this space.

Filing Status
Check only one box.

☐ Single ☐ Married filing jointly ☒ Married filing separately (MFS) ☐ Head of household (HOH) ☐ Qualifying surviving spouse (QSS)

If you checked the MFS box, enter the name of your spouse. If you checked the HOH or QSS box, enter the child's name if the qualifying person is a child but not your dependent.

Your first name and middle initial	Last name	Your social security number
MARRIED FILING SEPAR	ENTREPRENEUR	012-34-5678
If joint return, spouse's first name and middle initial	Last name	Spouse's social security number

Home address (number and street). If you have a P.O. box, see instructions	Apt. no.	
123 OPTIMISTIC LANE		**Presidential Election Campaign**

City, town, or post office. If you have a foreign address, also complete spaces below.	State	ZIP code
TOPEKA	KS	66611

Check here if you, or your spouse if filing jointly, want $3 to go to this fund. Checking a box below will not change your tax or refund.

Foreign country name	Foreign province/state/county	Foreign postal code

☐ You ☐ Spouse

Digital Assets
At any time during 2022, did you: (a) receive (as a reward, award, or payment for property or services); or (b) sell, exchange, gift, or otherwise dispose of a digital asset (or a financial interest in a digital asset)? (See instructions.) ☐ Yes ☒ No

Standard Deduction
Someone can claim: ☐ You as a dependent ☐ Your spouse as a dependent
☐ Spouse itemizes on a separate return or you were a dual-status alien

Age/Blindness You: ☐ Were born before January 2, 1958 ☐ Are blind **Spouse:** ☐ Was born before January 2, 1958 ☐ Is blind

Dependents (see instructions):
If more than four dependents, see instructions and check here ☐

(1) First name Last name	(2) Social security number	(3) Relationship to you	(4) Check the box if qualifies for (see instructions): Child tax credit	Credit for other dependents
KINSLEY ENTREPRENEUR	234-56-7890	Daughter	☒	☐
			☐	☐
			☐	☐
			☐	☐

Income

Attach Form(s) W-2 here. Also attach Forms W-2G and 1099-R if tax was withheld.

If you did not get a Form W-2, see instructions.

Attach Sch. B if required.

1a	Total amount from Form(s) W-2, box 1 (see instructions)			1a	
b	Household employee wages not reported on Form(s) W-2			1b	
c	Tip income not reported on line 1a (see instructions)			1c	
d	Medicaid waiver payments not reported on Form(s) W-2 (see instructions)			1d	
e	Taxable dependent care benefits from Form 2441, line 26			1e	
f	Employer-provided adoption benefits from Form 8839, line 29			1f	
g	Wages from Form 8919, line 6			1g	
h	Other earned income (see instructions)			1h	
i	Nontaxable combat pay election (see instructions)	1i			
z	Add lines 1a through 1h			1z	
2a	Tax-exempt interest	2a	b Taxable interest	2b	0.
3a	Qualified dividends	3a	b Ordinary dividends	3b	0.
4a	IRA distributions	4a	b Taxable amount	4b	
5a	Pensions and annuities	5a	b Taxable amount	5b	
6a	Social security benefits	6a	b Taxable amount	6b	
c	If you elect to use the lump-sum election method, check here (see instructions)		☐		
7	Capital gain or (loss). Attach Schedule D if required. If not required, check here		☐	7	
8	Other income from Schedule 1, line 10			8	384,136.
9	Add lines 1z, 2b, 3b, 4b, 5b, 6b, 7, and 8. This is your **total income**			9	384,136.
10	Adjustments to income from Schedule 1, line 26			10	14,258.
11	Subtract line 10 from line 9. This is your **adjusted gross income**			11	369,878.
12	Standard deduction or itemized deductions (from Schedule A)			12	12,950.
13	Qualified business income deduction from Form 8995 or Form 8995-A			13	37.
14	Add lines 12 and 13			14	12,987.
15	Subtract line 14 from line 11. If zero or less, enter -0-. This is your **taxable income**			15	356,891.

Standard Deduction for—
• Single or Married filing separately, $12,950.
• Married filing jointly or Qualifying surviving spouse, $25,900.
• Head of household, $19,400.
• If you checked any box under Standard Deduction, see instructions.

For Disclosure, Privacy Act, and Paperwork Reduction Act Notice, see separate instructions.

Form **1040** (2022)

Tax and Credits	16	Tax (see instructions). Check if any from Form(s): 1 ☐ 8814 2 ☐ 4972 3 ☐ _____			16	99,324.
	17	Amount from Schedule 2, line 3			17	
	18	Add lines 16 and 17			18	99,324.
	19	Child tax credit or credit for other dependents from Schedule 8812			19	
	20	Amount from Schedule 3, line 8			20	
	21	Add lines 19 and 20			21	
	22	Subtract line 21 from line 18. If zero or less, enter -0-			22	99,324.
	23	Other taxes, including self-employment tax, from Schedule 2, line 21			23	30,584.
	24	Add lines 22 and 23. This is your **total tax**			24	129,908.
Payments	25	Federal income tax withheld from:				
	a	Form(s) W-2		25a		
	b	Form(s) 1099		25b		
	c	Other forms (see instructions)		25c		
	d	Add lines 25a through 25c			25d	
If you have a qualifying child, attach Sch. EIC.	26	2022 estimated tax payments and amount applied from 2021 return			26	
	27	Earned income credit (EIC)		27		
	28	Additional child tax credit from Schedule 8812		28		
	29	American opportunity credit from Form 8863, line 8		29		
	30	Reserved for future use		30		
	31	Amount from Schedule 3, line 15		31		
	32	Add lines 27, 28, 29, and 31. These are your **total other payments and refundable credits**			32	
	33	Add lines 25d, 26, and 32. These are your **total payments**			33	
Refund	34	If line 33 is more than line 24, subtract line 24 from line 33. This is the amount you **overpaid**			34	
	35a	Amount of line 34 you want **refunded to you**. If Form 8888 is attached, check here ☐			35a	
Direct deposit? See instructions.	b	Routing number X X X X X X X X X c Type: ☐ Checking ☐ Savings				
	d	Account number X X X X X X X X X X X X X X X X X				
	36	Amount of line 34 you want **applied to your 2023 estimated tax**		36		
Amount You Owe	37	Subtract line 33 from line 24. This is the **amount you owe**. For details on how to pay, go to *www.irs.gov/Payments* or see instructions			37	129,908.
	38	Estimated tax penalty (see instructions)		38		

Third Party Designee	Do you want to allow another person to discuss this return with the IRS? See instructions		☐ **Yes.** Complete below.	☒ **No**
	Designee's name	Phone no.	Personal identification number (PIN)	

Sign Here

Under penalties of perjury, I declare that I have examined this return and accompanying schedules and statements, and to the best of my knowledge and belief, they are true, correct, and complete. Declaration of preparer (other than taxpayer) is based on all information of which preparer has any knowledge.

Your signature	Date	Your occupation ENTREPRENEUR	If the IRS sent you an Identity Protection PIN, enter it here (see inst.)
Joint return? See instructions. Keep a copy for your records.	Spouse's signature. If a joint return, **both** must sign.	Date	Spouse's occupation	If the IRS sent your spouse an Identity Protection PIN, enter it here (see inst.)
Phone no.		Email address	

Paid Preparer Use Only	Preparer's name Amy Rose Herrick	Preparer's signature Amy Rose Herrick	Date 07/27/2023	PTIN P00581983	Check if: ☒ Self-employed
	Firm's name Amy Rose Herrick			Phone no. (785) 224-8954	
	Firm's address 5020 State Solitude Christiansted VI 00820			Firm's EIN 74-2854800	

Go to *www.irs.gov/Form1040* for instructions and the latest information.   **BAA**   REV 07/10/23 PRO   Form **1040** (2022)

2022 tax table: married, filing separately

Tax rate	Taxable income bracket	Taxes owed
10%	$0 to $10,275.	10% of taxable income.
12%	$10,276 to $41,775.	$1,027.50 plus 12% of the amount over $10,275.
22%	$41,776 to $89,075.	$4,807.50 plus 22% of the amount over $41,775.
24%	$89,076 to $170,050.	$15,213.50 plus 24% of the amount over $89,075.
32%	$170,051 to $215,950.	$34,647.50 plus 32% of the amount over $170,050.
35%	$215,951 to $323,925.	$49,335.50 plus 35% of the amount over $215,950.
37%	$323,926 or more.	$87,126.75 plus 37% of the amount over $323,925.

In this final example, we will pretend that you are the "Married Filing Separately Entrepreneur" on the return inserted above.

On your hypothetical 2022 1040, line 15, the number $356,891 is your Federal taxable income after all deductions have been removed.

Using the chart above the first $10,275 is taxed at 10%.

the amount between $10,276 and $41,775 is taxed at 12%. Most of my clients are not going to notice much of a difference between 10% and 12% taxation.

You will recognize in your tax bill the next step up which is a 22% tax rate.

Now for our example we will also be maxing out the 22% tax bracket on income between $41,776 and $89,075.

Now for our example we will also be maxing out the 24% tax bracket on income between $89,076 and $170,050.

Now for our example we maxed out the 32% tax bracket on income between $170,051 and $215,950.

With income still climbing, we maxed out the 35% tax bracket on income between $215,951 and $323,925.

In the final tier we have income over $323,926 that is taxed at the top tax rate of 37%.

You will notice in our example the $356,891of taxable income puts $32,965 of income in the 37% tax bracket.

This means the first $32,965 in new deductions that we can identify will save us 37% on the dollar in federal income taxes.

Any new deductions over the $32,965 amount will have a 35% on the dollar in federal income tax reduction effect.

This is only part of the taxation picture if you are in a location that levies a state income tax. That tax rate would also apply to your tax savings depending on the brackets that may exist in your state using a chart that may look like the one above that is levied on the federal income tax portion.

When you are self-employed using a schedule C you would need to look on the 2022 return on the schedule one line 3 to see what your taxable income is specifically related to the profits in your business after all expenses have been deducted from your gross income.

But wait, we have a tax twist here behind the scenes.

Self-Employment Tax

Go to *www.irs.gov/ScheduleSE* for instructions and the latest information.

Attach to Form 1040, 1040-SR, or 1040-NR.

OMB No. 1545-0074

2022

Attachment
Sequence No. 17

Name of person with self-employment income (as shown on Form 1040, 1040-SR, or 1040-NR)	Social security number of person with **self-employment** income
MARRIED FILING SEPAR ENTREPRENEUR	012-34-5678

Part I — Self-Employment Tax

Note: If your only income subject to self-employment tax is **church employee income**, see instructions for how to report your income and the definition of church employee income.

A   If you are a minister, member of a religious order, or Christian Science practitioner **and** you filed Form 4361, but you had $400 or more of **other** net earnings from self-employment, check here and continue with Part I . . . . . ☐

Skip lines 1a and 1b if you use the farm optional method in Part II. See instructions.

1a	Net farm profit or (loss) from Schedule F, line 34, and farm partnerships, Schedule K-1 (Form 1065), box 14, code A	1a	
b	If you received social security retirement or disability benefits, enter the amount of Conservation Reserve Program payments included on Schedule F, line 4b, or listed on Schedule K-1 (Form 1065), box 20, code AH	1b	( )

Skip line 2 if you use the nonfarm optional method in Part II. See instructions.

2	Net profit or (loss) from Schedule C, line 31, and Schedule K-1 (Form 1065), box 14, code A (other than farming). See instructions for other income to report or if you are a minister or member of a religious order	2	384,136.
3	Combine lines 1a, 1b, and 2	3	384,136.
4a	If line 3 is more than zero, multiply line 3 by 92.35% (0.9235). Otherwise, enter amount from line 3	4a	354,750.
	Note: If line 4a is less than $400 due to Conservation Reserve Program payments on line 1b, see instructions.		
b	If you elect one or both of the optional methods, enter the total of lines 15 and 17 here	4b	
c	Combine lines 4a and 4b. If less than $400, **stop**; you don't owe self-employment tax. **Exception:** If less than $400 and you had **church employee income**, enter -0- and continue	4c	354,750.
5a	Enter your **church employee income** from Form W-2. See instructions for definition of church employee income 5a		
b	Multiply line 5a by 92.35% (0.9235). If less than $100, enter -0-	5b	0.
6	Add lines 4c and 5b	6	354,750.
7	Maximum amount of combined wages and self-employment earnings subject to social security tax or the 6.2% portion of the 7.65% railroad retirement (tier 1) tax for 2022	7	147,000
8a	Total social security wages and tips (total of boxes 3 and 7 on Form(s) W-2) and railroad retirement (tier 1) compensation. If $147,000 or more, skip lines 8b through 10, and go to line 11 8a		
b	Unreported tips subject to social security tax from Form 4137, line 10 8b		
c	Wages subject to social security tax from Form 8919, line 10 8c		
d	Add lines 8a, 8b, and 8c	8d	
9	Subtract line 8d from line 7. If zero or less, enter -0- here and on line 10 and go to line 11	9	147,000.
10	Multiply the **smaller** of line 6 or line 9 by 12.4% (0.124)	10	18,228.
11	Multiply line 6 by 2.9% (0.029)	11	10,288.
12	**Self-employment tax.** Add lines 10 and 11. Enter here and on **Schedule 2 (Form 1040), line 4**	12	28,516.
13	**Deduction for one-half of self-employment tax.** Multiply line 12 by 50% (0.50). Enter here and on **Schedule 1 (Form 1040), line 15** 13 14,258.		

Part II — Optional Methods To Figure Net Earnings (see instructions)

Farm Optional Method. You may use this method **only** if **(a)** your gross farm income[1] wasn't more than $9,060, **or (b)** your net farm profits[2] were less than $6,540.

14	Maximum income for optional methods	14	6,040
15	Enter the **smaller** of: two-thirds (2/3) of gross farm income[1] (not less than zero) or $6,040. Also, include this amount on line 4b above	15	

Nonfarm Optional Method. You may use this method **only** if **(a)** your net nonfarm profits[3] were less than $6,540 and also less than 72.189% of your gross nonfarm income,[4] **and (b)** you had net earnings from self-employment of at least $400 in 2 of the prior 3 years. **Caution:** You may use this method no more than five times.

16	Subtract line 15 from line 14	16	
17	Enter the **smaller** of: two-thirds (2/3) of gross nonfarm income[4] (not less than zero) or the amount on line 16. Also, include this amount on line 4b above	17	

[1] From Sch. F, line 9; and Sch. K-1 (Form 1065), box 14, code B.
[2] From Sch. F, line 34; and Sch. K-1 (Form 1065), box 14, code A—minus the amount you would have entered on line 1b had you not used the optional method.
[3] From Sch. C, line 31; and Sch. K-1 (Form 1065), box 14, code A.
[4] From Sch. C, line 7; and Sch. K-1 (Form 1065), box 14, code C.

For Paperwork Reduction Act Notice, see your tax return instructions.   BAA   REV 07/10/23 PRO   Schedule SE (Form 1040) 2022

This entrepreneur exceeded the $147,000 threshold for the Social Security tax levies to be imposed at 12.4% on self-employment. That means any taxable self-employment over $147,000 would not be subject to a 12.4% tax calculation.

However, all self-employment earnings with no ceiling are subject to the 2.9% Medicare levy.

Circling back to the example $356,891 taxable income for this "Married Filing Separately Entrepreneur", we can see the last dollars earned would be subject to 37% federal income taxes, 2.9% in Social Security taxes meaning we expect to lose 39.9% on the last dollars to taxation on our profits.

If you live in a state with state income taxes and we will pretend that that is a flat 5%, then on every profit dollar you would need to set aside 44.9% on the dollar for these three taxes levied. OUCH!

If you live in a state that also imposes a gross receipts taxes, that could be another percentage that is lost to taxation for this entrepreneur.

If this taxpayer were able to reduce their taxable income by only $20,000, at the 44.9% taxation rate that would be a reduction in taxes of $8,980 for only this tax year.

Are you doing anything else that reduces your costs by 44.5%?

Take my word for it, you will not gain all your tax savings in one area. Usually, it is a combination of several different areas that add up to a substantial difference on your return.

What is the average federal tax rate for this entrepreneur?

When I look at page two of the 1040 return, we see the taxes on the 1040 line 24 gives the amount of Federal taxes due of $129,908.

Tax and Credits	16	Tax (see instructions). Check if any from Form(s): 1 ☐ 8814 2 ☐ 4972 3 ☐ _____		16	99,324.
	17	Amount from Schedule 2, line 3		17	
	18	Add lines 16 and 17		18	99,324.
	19	Child tax credit or credit for other dependents from Schedule 8812		19	
	20	Amount from Schedule 3, line 8		20	
	21	Add lines 19 and 20		21	
	22	Subtract line 21 from line 18. If zero or less, enter -0-		22	99,324.
	23	Other taxes, including self-employment tax, from Schedule 2, line 21		23	30,584.
	24	Add lines 22 and 23. This is your **total tax**		24	129,908.
Payments	25	Federal income tax withheld from:			
	a	Form(s) W-2	25a		
	b	Form(s) 1099	25b		
	c	Other forms (see instructions)	25c		
	d	Add lines 25a through 25c		25d	
If you have a qualifying child, attach Sch. EIC.	26	2022 estimated tax payments and amount applied from 2021 return		26	
	27	Earned income credit (EIC)	27		
	28	Additional child tax credit from Schedule 8812	28		
	29	American opportunity credit from Form 8863, line 8	29		
	30	Reserved for future use	30		
	31	Amount from Schedule 3, line 15	31		
	32	Add lines 27, 28, 29, and 31. These are your **total other payments and refundable credits**		32	
	33	Add lines 25d, 26, and 32. These are your **total payments**		33	
Refund	34	If line 33 is more than line 24, subtract line 24 from line 33. This is the amount you **overpaid**		34	
	35a	Amount of line 34 you want **refunded to you**. If Form 8888 is attached, check here ☐		35a	
Direct deposit? See instructions.	b	Routing number XXXXXXXXX c Type: ☐ Checking ☐ Savings			
	d	Account number XXXXXXXXXXXXXXXXX			
	36	Amount of line 34 you want **applied to your 2023 estimated tax**	36		
Amount You Owe	37	Subtract line 33 from line 24. This is the **amount you owe**. For details on how to pay, go to *www.irs.gov/Payments* or see instructions		37	129,908.
	38	Estimated tax penalty (see instructions)	38		

Third Party Designee	Do you want to allow another person to discuss this return with the IRS? See instructions ☐ **Yes.** Complete below. ☒ **No**		
	Designee's name	Phone no.	Personal identification number (PIN)

Sign Here

Under penalties of perjury, I declare that I have examined this return and accompanying schedules and statements, and to the best of my knowledge and belief, they are true, correct, and complete. Declaration of preparer (other than taxpayer) is based on all information of which preparer has any knowledge.

	Your signature	Date	Your occupation ENTREPRENEUR	If the IRS sent you an Identity Protection PIN, enter it here (see inst.)
Joint return? See instructions. Keep a copy for your records.	Spouse's signature. If a joint return, **both** must sign.	Date	Spouse's occupation	If the IRS sent your spouse an Identity Protection PIN, enter it here (see inst.)
	Phone no.	Email address		

Paid Preparer Use Only	Preparer's name Amy Rose Herrick	Preparer's signature Amy Rose Herrick	Date 03/27/2023	PTIN P00581983	Check if: ☒ Self-employed
	Firm's name Amy Rose Herrick			Phone no. (785)224-8954	
	Firm's address 5020 State Solitude Christiansted VI 00820			Firm's EIN 74-2854800	

Go to *www.irs.gov/Form1040* for instructions and the latest information.   BAA   REV 07/10/23 PRO   Form **1040** (2022)

We take the $129,908 tax divided by the 1040-line 15 taxable income of $356,891 to reach an average tax rate across multiple tax brackets of 36.4%.

In the next chapter we will gather copies of your actual returns and some colored markers to begin working on your potential missed tax reduction opportunities.

CHAPTER 8

Using copies of your personal returns to uncover missed deductions

MONEY WITH AMY SERIES

SELF-EMPLOYED TAXES:
Unleashing Schedule C Deductions

I need to reinforce your understanding that every entry on your taxes is like a line of dominoes falling in different directions.

Every entry you put on the return has a ripple effect somewhere else that will decrease or increase the taxes you will pay.

Everyone wants to pay the least amount of taxes possible, agreed? Then you need to learn how to do that.

Here is where your participation in using your own tax returns begins and you start to identify all the areas where you are missing deductions and the resulting tax savings.

I need you to stop for a moment here.

WARNING: DO NOT USE YOUR ORIGINAL RETURN FOR THE COMING EXERCISES!!!!!

Print off a copy right now of your most recent tax return for this exercise before proceeding. 2022 is preferred, but not mandatory.

It is Ok, take your time to print off copies of all the pages as single sided sheets.

I do not want you to double side or double up pages today to save on printing costs. Full size sheets give you room to write notes along with your highlighted entries or to add notes on the reverse side of the form page you are highlighting.

I will be waiting right here when you are ready to move ahead.

This publication is based on the 2022 return, but even if the lines on the form change, the concepts will not.

Ready to go now? Good, let us focus our attention on finding the deductions to save you money by reducing your tax liabilities!

Next, with copies you can write on in front of you, I need you to grab a couple of highlighters too. I suggest you have three assorted colors to use for a visual reference key on the line-by-line entries we will go over in just a minute.

For example, you may be using green, yellow, and pink highlighters you had stashed in your drawer. If your children took them all, go take some back.

Colored pencils circling entries can work too. Use what you have.

You can use whatever colors you prefer. Just write the key with the color on the top page of the return so you do not forget the color key you are using.:

Green- a number is on the line. You are claiming something here.

Yellow- you have no entry on this line. This needs further scrutiny.

Pink- these are zero entries. There must be a reason there is a zero and the line is not empty, there is data hiding back there somewhere, and we need to see why it calculated a zero.

I suggest that you highlight all the line-by-line entries on your reference copy whether you have an amount, where you have a zero, or no entry at all to begin framing the potential discussion points about your unique situation as we move ahead.

It is a quick visual reference for you to see where you or your current preparer may have missed any potential tax savings opportunities on a recently filed return.

You may also need to discuss the highlighted line item in more depth to see if you are claiming everything you should claim on that line.

This is your last warning to stop right here until you have your copies and markers in hand before you resume reading and doing the exercises enclosed.

Now let us look over your return as a starting point and see if you have any possible missing entries that, if utilized, could potentially save you Federal income, State income and Social Security taxes that may have been missed on your return.

I am using a 2022 tax return page for reference. Other years numbering for these entries may be slightly different. We will be jumping around forms a bit.

2022 Form 1040 (A copy of the form is inserted at the end of this chapter for reference.)

Line 8- profits or losses from your Schedule C will be included in this number.

Line 13- QBI deduction is calculated on form 8995.

Line 23- this is the amount of Social Security taxes due calculated on form SE.

Line 27 will only apply if your income meets the guidelines and is calculated on Schedule EIC.

I have seen this refundable tax credit happen as a surprise one-time occurrence. could happen two years in a row if you are living off savings trying to build a profitable business.

An unexpected EIC tax credit could happen to you in a year with large losses and transitions into entrepreneurship that deflate income in a single tax year when all those tax dominoes, as I mentioned, fall in a sequence that is triggered for taxpayers who have never received it before.

In any case, I tell taxpayers to count this extra refund as a gift, because it may never happen again. Do not count on it.

Line 31 may apply from Schedule 3 entries.

Look at the bottom of the return on page two.

If you paid someone to do the return, and they did not include their name and contact information, you have an issue.

They do not want to be recognized or to be identified for the work completed on the returns you hold in your hands you paid them to do as a professional.

If you see the words "Self- Prepared" and you did not prepare it yourself, are you surprised at this revelation? This is a common red flag for non-professionals you may never have known to look for prior to submitting your tax returns. In case you skipped past a few chapters to be here instead, refer to Chapter 2 for more information on this key point.

Paid Preparer Use Only	Preparer's name	Preparer's signature	Date	PTIN	Check if: ☐ Self-employed
	Firm's name			Phone no.	
	Firm's address			Firm's EIN	

Go to www.irs.gov/Form1040 for instructions and the latest information.

Form **1040** (2022)

Form 1040

Department of the Treasury—Internal Revenue Service

U.S. Individual Income Tax Return

2022

OMB No. 1545-0074 | IRS Use Only—Do not write or staple in this space.

Filing Status
Check only one box.

☐ Single ☐ Married filing jointly ☐ Married filing separately (MFS) ☐ Head of household (HOH) ☐ Qualifying surviving spouse (QSS)

If you checked the MFS box, enter the name of your spouse. If you checked the HOH or QSS box, enter the child's name if the qualifying person is a child but not your dependent:

Your first name and middle initial	Last name	Your social security number
If joint return, spouse's first name and middle initial	Last name	Spouse's social security number

Home address (number and street). If you have a P.O. box, see instructions.		Apt. no.
City, town, or post office. If you have a foreign address, also complete spaces below.	State	ZIP code
Foreign country name	Foreign province/state/county	Foreign postal code

Presidential Election Campaign
Check here if you, or your spouse if filing jointly, want $3 to go to this fund. Checking a box below will not change your tax or refund.
☐ You ☐ Spouse

Digital Assets
At any time during 2022, did you: (a) receive (as a reward, award, or payment for property or services); or (b) sell, exchange, gift, or otherwise dispose of a digital asset (or a financial interest in a digital asset)? (See instructions.) ☐ Yes ☐ No

Standard Deduction
Someone can claim: ☐ You as a dependent ☐ Your spouse as a dependent
☐ Spouse itemizes on a separate return or you were a dual-status alien

Age/Blindness You: ☐ Were born before January 2, 1958 ☐ Are blind **Spouse:** ☐ Was born before January 2, 1958 ☐ Is blind

Dependents (see instructions):
If more than four dependents, see instructions and check here . . ☐

(1) First name Last name	(2) Social security number	(3) Relationship to you	(4) Check the box if qualifies for (see instructions):	
			Child tax credit	Credit for other dependents
			☐	☐
			☐	☐
			☐	☐
			☐	☐

Income

Attach Form(s) W-2 here. Also attach Forms W-2G and 1099-R if tax was withheld.

If you did not get a Form W-2, see instructions.

Attach Sch. B if required.

1a	Total amount from Form(s) W-2, box 1 (see instructions)	1a	
b	Household employee wages not reported on Form(s) W-2	1b	
c	Tip income not reported on line 1a (see instructions)	1c	
d	Medicaid waiver payments not reported on Form(s) W-2 (see instructions) . .	1d	
e	Taxable dependent care benefits from Form 2441, line 26	1e	
f	Employer-provided adoption benefits from Form 8839, line 29	1f	
g	Wages from Form 8919, line 6	1g	
h	Other earned income (see instructions)	1h	
i	Nontaxable combat pay election (see instructions)	1i		
z	Add lines 1a through 1h	1z	

2a	Tax-exempt interest . . .	2a		b	Taxable interest	2b	
3a	Qualified dividends . . .	3a		b	Ordinary dividends . . .	3b	
4a	IRA distributions	4a		b	Taxable amount	4b	
5a	Pensions and annuities . .	5a		b	Taxable amount	5b	
6a	Social security benefits . .	6a		b	Taxable amount	6b	

Standard Deduction for—
• Single or Married filing separately, $12,950
• Married filing jointly or Qualifying surviving spouse, $25,900
• Head of household, $19,400
• If you checked any box under Standard Deduction, see instructions.

c	If you elect to use the lump-sum election method, check here (see instructions) . . ☐	
7	Capital gain or (loss). Attach Schedule D if required. If not required, check here . . ☐	7
8	Other income from Schedule 1, line 10	8
9	Add lines 1z, 2b, 3b, 4b, 5b, 6b, 7, and 8. This is your **total income**	9
10	Adjustments to income from Schedule 1, line 26	10
11	Subtract line 10 from line 9. This is your **adjusted gross income**	11
12	**Standard deduction or itemized deductions** (from Schedule A)	12
13	Qualified business income deduction from Form 8995 or Form 8995-A	13
14	Add lines 12 and 13	14
15	Subtract line 14 from line 11. If zero or less, enter -0-. This is your **taxable income** . .	15

For Disclosure, Privacy Act, and Paperwork Reduction Act Notice, see separate instructions.

Cat. No. 11320B

Form **1040** (2022)

Tax and Credits	16	**Tax** (see instructions). Check if any from Form(s): **1** ☐ 8814 **2** ☐ 4972 **3** ☐ _____		16	
	17	Amount from Schedule 2, line 3		17	
	18	Add lines 16 and 17		18	
	19	Child tax credit or credit for other dependents from Schedule 8812		19	
	20	Amount from Schedule 3, line 8		20	
	21	Add lines 19 and 20		21	
	22	Subtract line 21 from line 18. If zero or less, enter -0-		22	
	23	Other taxes, including self-employment tax, from Schedule 2, line 21		23	
	24	Add lines 22 and 23. This is your **total tax**		24	
Payments	25	Federal income tax withheld from:			
	a	Form(s) W-2	25a		
	b	Form(s) 1099	25b		
	c	Other forms (see instructions)	25c		
	d	Add lines 25a through 25c		25d	
If you have a qualifying child, attach Sch. EIC.	26	2022 estimated tax payments and amount applied from 2021 return		26	
	27	Earned income credit (EIC)	27		
	28	Additional child tax credit from Schedule 8812	28		
	29	American opportunity credit from Form 8863, line 8	29		
	30	Reserved for future use	30		
	31	Amount from Schedule 3, line 15	31		
	32	Add lines 27, 28, 29, and 31. These are your **total other payments and refundable credits**		32	
	33	Add lines 25d, 26, and 32. These are your **total payments**		33	
Refund	34	If line 33 is more than line 24, subtract line 24 from line 33. This is the amount you **overpaid**		34	
	35a	Amount of line 34 you want **refunded to you**. If Form 8888 is attached, check here ☐		35a	
Direct deposit? See instructions.	b	Routing number [ ] **c** Type: ☐ Checking ☐ Savings			
	d	Account number [ ]			
	36	Amount of line 34 you want **applied to your 2023 estimated tax**	36		
Amount You Owe	37	Subtract line 33 from line 24. This is the **amount you owe**. For details on how to pay, go to *www.irs.gov/Payments* or see instructions		37	
	38	Estimated tax penalty (see instructions)	38		

Third Party Designee	Do you want to allow another person to discuss this return with the IRS? See instructions . . . . ☐ **Yes.** Complete below. ☐ **No**		
	Designee's name	Phone no.	Personal identification number (PIN) [ ]

Sign Here	Under penalties of perjury, I declare that I have examined this return and accompanying schedules and statements, and to the best of my knowledge and belief, they are true, correct, and complete. Declaration of preparer (other than taxpayer) is based on all information of which preparer has any knowledge.			
	Your signature	Date	Your occupation	If the IRS sent you an Identity Protection PIN, enter it here (see inst.) [ ]
Joint return? See instructions. Keep a copy for your records.	Spouse's signature. If a joint return, **both** must sign.	Date	Spouse's occupation	If the IRS sent your spouse an Identity Protection PIN, enter it here (see inst.) [ ]
	Phone no.	Email address		

Paid Preparer Use Only	Preparer's name	Preparer's signature	Date	PTIN	Check if: ☐ Self-employed
	Firm's name			Phone no.	
	Firm's address			Firm's EIN	

Go to *www.irs.gov/Form1040* for instructions and the latest information.   Form **1040** (2022)

Now let us get started changing your income tax in the future and continue putting those copies and markers to use I asked you to have ready for the next steps in the following chapter starting with Schedule 1.

MONEY WITH AMY SERIES

SELF-EMPLOYED TAXES:
Unleashing Schedule C Deductions

<u>2022 Schedule 1</u> (A copy of the form is inserted at the end of this chapter for reference.)

Line 3- This will be the total profits from all Schedule C pages in the returns whether you have one Schedule C or more combined.

Line 13- this is dependent on whether you have a H.S.A. medical plan or not for your health insurance coverage. The best health insurance plan for you is not a discussion I will cover here.

Line 15- If you had a profit on your Schedule C, or all Schedule C's combined, on form SE, the amount of Social Security taxes is calculated and placed here. If you are married and you are both self-employed, you will each have your own schedule SE.

Line 16 & 20 - Do you have a retirement plan in place? What account title is best for you is a different discussion than we will have here. Whether you should be funding these accounts with pre-tax or after-tax plan contributions is another discussion based on your tax bracket now and expected over time as you learn to "work the brackets" covered in a prior chapter.

Line 17- If you have health, air ambulance, supplemental insurance like cancer, vision or dental coverage, Medicare Part B or D that are NOT subsidized by an employer, how you use this deduction line is important to you.

You may be much better served by putting eligible premium payments here instead of lumping into Schedule A deductions where they may be useless to you when you cannot itemize.

SCHEDULE 1
(Form 1040)

Department of the Treasury
Internal Revenue Service

Additional Income and Adjustments to Income

Attach to Form 1040, 1040-SR, or 1040-NR.
Go to *www.irs.gov/Form1040* for instructions and the latest information.

OMB No. 1545-0074

2022

Attachment
Sequence No. **01**

Name(s) shown on Form 1040, 1040-SR, or 1040-NR

Your social security number

Part I   Additional Income

1	Taxable refunds, credits, or offsets of state and local income taxes	**1**	
2a	Alimony received	**2a**	
b	Date of original divorce or separation agreement (see instructions):		
3	Business income or (loss). Attach Schedule C	**3**	
4	Other gains or (losses). Attach Form 4797	**4**	
5	Rental real estate, royalties, partnerships, S corporations, trusts, etc. Attach Schedule E	**5**	
6	Farm income or (loss). Attach Schedule F	**6**	
7	Unemployment compensation	**7**	
8	Other income:		
a	Net operating loss	**8a** ( )	
b	Gambling	**8b**	
c	Cancellation of debt	**8c**	
d	Foreign earned income exclusion from Form 2555	**8d** ( )	
e	Income from Form 8853	**8e**	
f	Income from Form 8889	**8f**	
g	Alaska Permanent Fund dividends	**8g**	
h	Jury duty pay	**8h**	
i	Prizes and awards	**8i**	
j	Activity not engaged in for profit income	**8j**	
k	Stock options	**8k**	
l	Income from the rental of personal property if you engaged in the rental for profit but were not in the business of renting such property	**8l**	
m	Olympic and Paralympic medals and USOC prize money (see instructions)	**8m**	
n	Section 951(a) inclusion (see instructions)	**8n**	
o	Section 951A(a) inclusion (see instructions)	**8o**	
p	Section 461(l) excess business loss adjustment	**8p**	
q	Taxable distributions from an ABLE account (see instructions)	**8q**	
r	Scholarship and fellowship grants not reported on Form W-2	**8r**	
s	Nontaxable amount of Medicaid waiver payments included on Form 1040, line 1a or 1d	**8s** ( )	
t	Pension or annuity from a nonqualifed deferred compensation plan or a nongovernmental section 457 plan	**8t**	
u	Wages earned while incarcerated	**8u**	
z	Other income. List type and amount:	**8z**	
9	Total other income. Add lines 8a through 8z	**9**	
10	Combine lines 1 through 7 and 9. Enter here and on Form 1040, 1040-SR, or 1040-NR, line 8	**10**	

For Paperwork Reduction Act Notice, see your tax return instructions.   Cat. No. 71479F   Schedule 1 (Form 1040) 2022

Part II   Adjustments to Income

11	Educator expenses	11
12	Certain business expenses of reservists, performing artists, and fee-basis government officials. Attach Form 2106	12
13	Health savings account deduction. Attach Form 8889	13
14	Moving expenses for members of the Armed Forces. Attach Form 3903	14
15	Deductible part of self-employment tax. Attach Schedule SE	15
16	Self-employed SEP, SIMPLE, and qualified plans	16
17	Self-employed health insurance deduction	17
18	Penalty on early withdrawal of savings	18
19a	Alimony paid	19a
b	Recipient's SSN	
c	Date of original divorce or separation agreement (see instructions): _____	
20	IRA deduction	20
21	Student loan interest deduction	21
22	Reserved for future use	22
23	Archer MSA deduction	23
24	Other adjustments:	
a	Jury duty pay (see instructions)	24a
b	Deductible expenses related to income reported on line 8l from the rental of personal property engaged in for profit	24b
c	Nontaxable amount of the value of Olympic and Paralympic medals and USOC prize money reported on line 8m	24c
d	Reforestation amortization and expenses	24d
e	Repayment of supplemental unemployment benefits under the Trade Act of 1974	24e
f	Contributions to section 501(c)(18)(D) pension plans	24f
g	Contributions by certain chaplains to section 403(b) plans	24g
h	Attorney fees and court costs for actions involving certain unlawful discrimination claims (see instructions)	24h
i	Attorney fees and court costs you paid in connection with an award from the IRS for information you provided that helped the IRS detect tax law violations	24i
j	Housing deduction from Form 2555	24j
k	Excess deductions of section 67(e) expenses from Schedule K-1 (Form 1041)	24k
z	Other adjustments. List type and amount: _____	24z
25	Total other adjustments. Add lines 24a through 24z	25
26	Add lines 11 through 23 and 25. These are your **adjustments to income**. Enter here and on Form 1040 or 1040-SR, line 10, or Form 1040-NR, line 10a	26

Now let us get started changing your income tax in the future and continue putting those copies and markers to use I asked you to have ready for the next steps in the following chapter addressing Schedule 2.

CHAPTER 10

Schedule 2

MONEY WITH AMY SERIES

SELF-EMPLOYED TAXES:
Unleashing Schedule C Deductions

Line 4- this is where the Social Security tax portion amount calculated on the Schedule SE is placed.

SCHEDULE 2 (Form 1040) Department of the Treasury Internal Revenue Service	**Additional Taxes** Attach to Form 1040, 1040-SR, or 1040-NR. Go to *www.irs.gov/Form1040* for instructions and the latest information.	OMB No. 1545-0074 2022 Attachment Sequence No. 02

Name(s) shown on Form 1040, 1040-SR, or 1040-NR | Your social security number

Part I Tax

1	Alternative minimum tax. Attach Form 6251	1	
2	Excess advance premium tax credit repayment. Attach Form 8962	2	
3	Add lines 1 and 2. Enter here and on Form 1040, 1040-SR, or 1040-NR, line 17 . .	3	

Part II Other Taxes

4	Self-employment tax. Attach Schedule SE		4	
5	Social security and Medicare tax on unreported tip income. Attach Form 4137	5		
6	Uncollected social security and Medicare tax on wages. Attach Form 8919	6		
7	Total additional social security and Medicare tax. Add lines 5 and 6		7	
8	Additional tax on IRAs or other tax-favored accounts. Attach Form 5329 if required. If not required, check here . . . . ☐		8	
9	Household employment taxes. Attach Schedule H		9	
10	Repayment of first-time homebuyer credit. Attach Form 5405 if required		10	
11	Additional Medicare Tax. Attach Form 8959		11	
12	Net investment income tax. Attach Form 8960		12	
13	Uncollected social security and Medicare or RRTA tax on tips or group-term life insurance from Form W-2, box 12		13	
14	Interest on tax due on installment income from the sale of certain residential lots and timeshares		14	
15	Interest on the deferred tax on gain from certain installment sales with a sales price over $150,000		15	
16	Recapture of low-income housing credit. Attach Form 8611		16	

(continued on page 2)

For Paperwork Reduction Act Notice, see your tax return instructions. Cat. No. 71478U Schedule 2 (Form 1040) 2022

Now let us get started changing your income tax in the future and continue putting those copies and markers to use I asked you to have ready for the next steps in the following chapter addressing Schedule 3.

MONEY WITH AMY SERIES

SELF-EMPLOYED TAXES:
Unleashing Schedule C Deductions

Line 4- This is calculated on form 8880 and will only apply if your income and contributions meet the guidelines.

I have seen this tax credit happen as a surprise one-time occurrence in a year with large losses and transitions into entrepreneurship that deflate income in a single tax year.

This could happen unexpectedly when all those tax dominoes I mentioned before fall in a sequence that this tax credit triggered for taxpayers who have never received it before.

If you file early, we see you are eligible for this tax credit, and you have not put money in a retirement account, you can trigger it if you put eligible deposits in by IRS filing deadlines.

Line 11- if you had W2 income in addition to self-employment, or you changed W2 employers in the same tax year, you may have overpaid your Social Security taxes obligations via payroll deductions. This is a way to have that excess contribution returned to you.

In the next chapter we talk about the importance of the sequence of profits and losses when it comes to having your endeavor reclassified as a hobby instead of a business.

Additional Credits and Payments

Attach to Form 1040, 1040-SR, or 1040-NR.
Go to *www.irs.gov/Form1040* for instructions and the latest information.

OMB No. 1545-0074

2022

Attachment
Sequence No. 03

Name(s) shown on Form 1040, 1040-SR, or 1040-NR

Your social security number

Part I — Nonrefundable Credits

1	Foreign tax credit. Attach Form 1116 if required	1	
2	Credit for child and dependent care expenses from Form 2441, line 11. Attach Form 2441	2	
3	Education credits from Form 8863, line 19	3	
4	Retirement savings contributions credit. Attach Form 8880	4	
5	Residential energy credits. Attach Form 5695	5	
6	Other nonrefundable credits:		
a	General business credit. Attach Form 3800	6a	
b	Credit for prior year minimum tax. Attach Form 8801	6b	
c	Adoption credit. Attach Form 8839	6c	
d	Credit for the elderly or disabled. Attach Schedule R	6d	
e	Alternative motor vehicle credit. Attach Form 8910	6e	
f	Qualified plug-in motor vehicle credit. Attach Form 8936 . . .	6f	
g	Mortgage interest credit. Attach Form 8396	6g	
h	District of Columbia first-time homebuyer credit. Attach Form 8859	6h	
i	Qualified electric vehicle credit. Attach Form 8834	6i	
j	Alternative fuel vehicle refueling property credit. Attach Form 8911	6j	
k	Credit to holders of tax credit bonds. Attach Form 8912 . . .	6k	
l	Amount on Form 8978, line 14. See instructions	6l	
z	Other nonrefundable credits. List type and amount: _____	6z	
7	Total other nonrefundable credits. Add lines 6a through 6z	7	
8	Add lines 1 through 5 and 7. Enter here and on Form 1040, 1040-SR, or 1040-NR, line 20	8	

(continued on page 2)

For Paperwork Reduction Act Notice, see your tax return instructions.   Cat. No. 71480G   Schedule 3 (Form 1040) 2022

57

Part II	Other Payments and Refundable Credits		
9	Net premium tax credit. Attach Form 8962	9	
10	Amount paid with request for extension to file (see instructions)	10	
11	Excess social security and tier 1 RRTA tax withheld	11	
12	Credit for federal tax on fuels. Attach Form 4136	12	
13	Other payments or refundable credits:		
a	Form 2439 . . . . **13a**		
b	Credit for qualified sick and family leave wages paid in 2022 from Schedule(s) H for leave taken before April 1, 2021 . . . . . . **13b**		
c	Reserved for future use **13c**		
d	Credit for repayment of amounts included in income from earlier years **13d**		
e	Reserved for future use **13e**		
f	Deferred amount of net 965 tax liability (see instructions) . . . **13f**		
g	Reserved for future use **13g**		
h	Credit for qualified sick and family leave wages paid in 2022 from Schedule(s) H for leave taken after March 31, 2021, and before October 1, 2021 . . . . **13h**		
z	Other payments or refundable credits. List type and amount: **13z**		
14	Total other payments or refundable credits. Add lines 13a through 13z	14	
15	Add lines 9 through 12 and 14. Enter here and on Form 1040, 1040-SR, or 1040-NR, line 31	15	

Now we need to learn next about the rolling two out of five rule in the next chapter, and why you need to track it.

CHAPTER 12

Understanding the 2 of 5 rolling year rule for a business versus a hobby

MONEY WITH AMY SERIES

SELF-EMPLOYED TAXES:
Unleashing Schedule C Deductions

Now is the perfect time to discuss the two out of five rolling years rule of thumb when we are determining whether an endeavor is a business, or it is a hobby.

This is a general rule of thumb that any business should be able to post a profit in two out of every five rolling years or more.

I will add a caveat here that with the unprecedented closures and changes that occurred as a result of COVID-19 coupled in some areas with natural disasters it has yet to be seen how businesses that exceeded this guideline over the last few tax filing years will be treated with these back-to-back unusual business interrupting one-time events that caused untold numbers of business to struggle to even keep the doors open.

Millions of businesses relied on taking out SBA or EIDL loans to remain afloat during those challenging times.

When I think about the two out of five-year rolling rule it does not really matter what the sequence is as long as you do not violate the profit in two out of any five years rule.

If you look at the sequence of numbers that I will put below as examples, you can see what I mean when I say that the sequence is not as important as the results that do not violate the profits in two out of five years.

Winning the Profit and Loss Game to Protect prior Deductions

Examples of 2 out of 5 rolling years within guidelines models:

2023 Could be a profit or a loss and not be construed a hobby when 2018 falls off

2022 Loss

2021 Profit

2020 Profit

2019 Profit

2018 Loss

2026 Could be a profit or a loss and not be construed a hobby when 2021 falls off

2025 Must be a profit to not be construed a hobby when 2020 falls off

2024 Must be a profit to not be construed a hobby when 2019 falls off

2023 Must be a profit to not be construed a hobby when 2018 falls off

2022 Loss

2021 Loss

2020 Profit

2019 Profit

2018 Profit

Examples of 2 out of 5 rolling years outside of guidelines models are in danger of having deductions disallowed in prior years if reclassified as a hobby and resulting new tax liabilities, penalties and interest would be triggered:

2022 Loss

2021 Loss

2020 Profit

2019 Loss

2018 Loss

2022 Profit

2021 Loss

2020 Profit

2019 Loss

2018 Loss

It is important to note this rule is just one of many rules or guidelines that could apply if you were challenged on this issue of a business or a hobby for claimed deductions. It is a fast point of reference to see if you are entering a potential audit danger zone never realizing a profit.

There are at this writing, nine things to consider on the IRS website page when you look at the overall business versus a hobby picture. Here is a link for reference and an excerpt: https://www.irs.gov/newsroom/earning-side-income-is-it-a-hobby-or-a-business

- Whether the activity is carried out in a businesslike manner and the taxpayer maintains complete and accurate books and records.

- Whether the time and effort the taxpayer puts into the activity show they intend to make it profitable.

- Whether they depend on income from the activity for their livelihood.

- Whether any losses are due to circumstances beyond the taxpayer's control or are normal for the startup phase of their type of business.

- Whether they change methods of operation to improve profitability.

- Whether the taxpayer and their advisors have the knowledge needed to carry out the activity as a successful business.

- Whether the taxpayer was successful in making a profit in similar activities in the past.

- Whether the activity makes a profit in some years and how much profit it makes.

- Whether the taxpayers can expect to make a future profit from the appreciation of the assets used in the activity.

In the next Chapter we get started on the Schedule C form where we will determine your eligible Income and deductions.

CHAPTER 13

Schedule C

MONEY WITH AMY SERIES

SELF-EMPLOYED TAXES:
Unleashing Schedule C Deductions

<u>Schedule C:</u> (A copy of the form is inserted at the end of this chapter for reference on all chapters related to this form.)

Deductions clearly labeled are easy to figure out.

Not all deductions on the Schedule C apply to every self-employed endeavor.

I am only targeting the Schedule C form line entries in the coming chapters in this book I see missed or underused the most.

Usually, the disconnect in claiming the deductions you are entitled to is because of a lack of understanding, which can hold hands with a failure to keep good records to structure tax deductions correctly and to your advantage.

Do you see how categories listed on the form inserted below are in the titling self-explanatory? No need to waste our time on those.

In our next chapter we begin the learning process about individual lines on the Schedule C form.

SCHEDULE C
(Form 1040)

Department of the Treasury
Internal Revenue Service

Profit or Loss From Business
(Sole Proprietorship)

Go to *www.irs.gov/ScheduleC* for instructions and the latest information.

Attach to Form 1040, 1040-SR, 1040-NR, or 1041; partnerships must generally file Form 1065.

OMB No. 1545-0074

2022

Attachment
Sequence No. **09**

Name of proprietor | Social security number (SSN)

A Principal business or profession, including product or service (see instructions) | **B** Enter code from instructions

C Business name. If no separate business name, leave blank. | **D** Employer ID number (EIN) (see instr.)

E Business address (including suite or room no.)

City, town or post office, state, and ZIP code

F Accounting method: **(1)** ☐ Cash **(2)** ☐ Accrual **(3)** ☐ Other (specify)

G Did you "materially participate" in the operation of this business during 2022? If "No," see instructions for limit on losses . . ☐ Yes ☐ No

H If you started or acquired this business during 2022, check here . . . . ☐

I Did you make any payments in 2022 that would require you to file Form(s) 1099? See instructions . . . . ☐ Yes ☐ No

J If "Yes," did you or will you file required Form(s) 1099? . . . . ☐ Yes ☐ No

Part I   Income

1	Gross receipts or sales. See instructions for line 1 and check the box if this income was reported to you on Form W-2 and the "Statutory employee" box on that form was checked . . . . ☐	1	
2	Returns and allowances	2	
3	Subtract line 2 from line 1	3	
4	Cost of goods sold (from line 42)	4	
5	**Gross profit.** Subtract line 4 from line 3	5	
6	Other income, including federal and state gasoline or fuel tax credit or refund (see instructions) . . .	6	
7	**Gross income.** Add lines 5 and 6	7	

Part II   Expenses. Enter expenses for business use of your home **only** on line 30.

8	Advertising	8		18	Office expense (see instructions) .	18	
9	Car and truck expenses (see instructions) . . .	9		19	Pension and profit-sharing plans .	19	
				20	Rent or lease (see instructions):		
10	Commissions and fees	10		a	Vehicles, machinery, and equipment	20a	
11	Contract labor (see instructions)	11		b	Other business property . . .	20b	
12	Depletion	12		21	Repairs and maintenance . .	21	
13	Depreciation and section 179 expense deduction (not included in Part III) (see instructions) . . .	13		22	Supplies (not included in Part III)	22	
				23	Taxes and licenses	23	
				24	Travel and meals:		
14	Employee benefit programs (other than on line 19) .	14		a	Travel	24a	
15	Insurance (other than health)	15		b	Deductible meals (see instructions)	24b	
16	Interest (see instructions):			25	Utilities	25	
a	Mortgage (paid to banks, etc.)	16a		26	Wages (less employment credits)	26	
b	Other	16b		27a	Other expenses (from line 48) .	27a	
17	Legal and professional services	17		b	**Reserved for future use** . .	27b	

28	**Total expenses** before expenses for business use of home. Add lines 8 through 27a	28	
29	Tentative profit or (loss). Subtract line 28 from line 7	29	
30	Expenses for business use of your home. Do not report these expenses elsewhere. Attach Form 8829 unless using the simplified method. See instructions. **Simplified method filers only:** Enter the total square footage of (a) your home: _____ and (b) the part of your home used for business: _____. Use the Simplified Method Worksheet in the instructions to figure the amount to enter on line 30	30	
31	**Net profit or (loss).** Subtract line 30 from line 29. • If a profit, enter on both **Schedule 1 (Form 1040), line 3**, and on **Schedule SE, line 2.** (If you checked the box on line 1, see instructions.) Estates and trusts, enter on **Form 1041, line 3.** • If a loss, you **must** go to line 32.	31	
32	If you have a loss, check the box that describes your investment in this activity. See instructions. • If you checked 32a, enter the loss on both **Schedule 1 (Form 1040), line 3**, and on **Schedule SE, line 2.** (If you checked the box on line 1, see the line 31 instructions.) Estates and trusts, enter on **Form 1041, line 3.** • If you checked 32b, you **must** attach **Form 6198.** Your loss may be limited.	32a ☐ All investment is at risk. 32b ☐ Some investment is not at risk.

For Paperwork Reduction Act Notice, see the separate instructions.   Cat. No. 11334P   Schedule C (Form 1040) 2022

Part III **Cost of Goods Sold** (see instructions)

33 Method(s) used to value closing inventory. a ☐ Cost b ☐ Lower of cost or market c ☐ Other (attach explanation)

34 Was there any change in determining quantities, costs, or valuations between opening and closing inventory? If "Yes," attach explanation . . . . ☐ Yes ☐ No

35	Inventory at beginning of year. If different from last year's closing inventory, attach explanation	35
36	Purchases less cost of items withdrawn for personal use	36
37	Cost of labor. Do not include any amounts paid to yourself	37
38	Materials and supplies	38
39	Other costs	39
40	Add lines 35 through 39	40
41	Inventory at end of year	41
42	**Cost of goods sold.** Subtract line 41 from line 40. Enter the result here and on line 4	42

Part IV **Information on Your Vehicle.** Complete this part **only** if you are claiming car or truck expenses on line 9 and are not required to file Form 4562 for this business. See the instructions for line 13 to find out if you must file Form 4562.

43 When did you place your vehicle in service for business purposes? (month/day/year) / /

44 Of the total number of miles you drove your vehicle during 2022, enter the number of miles you used your vehicle for:

a Business _____ b Commuting (see instructions) _____ c Other _____

45 Was your vehicle available for personal use during off-duty hours? . . . . ☐ Yes ☐ No

46 Do you (or your spouse) have another vehicle available for personal use? . . . . . ☐ Yes ☐ No

47a Do you have evidence to support your deduction? . . . . ☐ Yes ☐ No

b If "Yes," is the evidence written? . . . . ☐ Yes ☐ No

Part V **Other Expenses.** List below business expenses not included on lines 8–26 or line 30.

48 Total other expenses. Enter here and on line 27a	48

In the following chapters we will be discussing many lines one by one starting with line 6.

CHAPTER 14

Schedule C, line 6 Bartering

MONEY WITH AMY SERIES

SELF-EMPLOYED TAXES:
Unleashing Schedule C Deductions

Line 6- Do you engage in bartering? If you do not receive a tax form from a bartering network to report elsewhere on the return, your bartering income should be reported here.

Yes, I know, you will be surprised to learn bartering income is a taxable event.

Bartering for goods or services can also be a deduction.

This method of economic exchange is a deeper discussion topic you need to have with a tax professional.

Is it profitable for you? Here is a quick worksheet to help you determine profitability of bartering in a network.

EXERCISE: Is a barter transaction profitable for you to consider?

Hard cost of the item you will barter $_____

Trading fee to sell item   +_____

Trading fee to purchase another item   +_____

Monthly trading maintenance fee   +_____

Total hard cost of the transaction $_____

VS

Value of the barter in your account $_____

**Gain or loss from barter transaction
for this product or service**   +/-_____

Decision time: Proceed with the Barter to make a profit: YES OR NO

In the following chapters we will be discussing many lines one by one with the next discussion point being line 9.

CHAPTER 15

Schedule C, line 9

MONEY WITH AMY SERIES

SELF-EMPLOYED TAXES:
Unleashing Schedule C Deductions

Line 9 is related to page 2 of the Schedule C part IV.

Do you know what would create the largest tax deduction here when you use a vehicle for business purposes?

Are you better off claiming the standard mileage deduction or your actual operating expenses percentage on this line related to business travel necessary to run your business?

I suggest you seek out qualified tax help on this one to know what is most advantageous for you.

Option #1.

The standard mileage rate method is a flat rate set per mile for business related travel. It is important to keep your mileage log by day and month. Why? We have experienced tax years that have had two different mileage rates imposed. For example, one rate applied for business miles that were incurred from 1/2 to 6/30 of a tax year. The second rate applied to business miles that were incurred from 7/1 – 12/31. Will there be two rates in future years? Who knows?

Option #2

You will still need to keep track of your mileage, unless you use the vehicle 100% for business

Using this percentage method, you will be able to take all the expenses for a vehicle and prorate it between business miles, which will be deductible and personal miles, which will not be deductible

To give you an idea of how valuable this method can be in the right circumstances let us talk a little bit about all the operating expenses that would come into play using this method

Insurance
Taxes and tags
Gasoline
Tires
Oil changes
Repairs
The interest on a car loan
Depreciation
Car washes

Whatever it takes to maintain and operate this vehicle on an annual basis will be the basic number you will be working with

For example, let us pretend that you have 10,000 business miles a year in the same vehicle as a self-employed person. You have 10,000 personal miles.

This means you have 50% business use on this vehicle

Let us pretend that the annual mileage rate for this tax year is $.50 per mile

Under the standard mileage rate, I would take the $.50 per mile times the 10,000 business miles which gives me a deduction of $5,000 on my Schedule C line 9.

In contrast, I decided to look at the actual operating expense method to see what the deduction may be there.

In this case, when I add up all the various operating expenses of the vehicle, let us pretend that it cost me $15,000 for the items listed above.

I still have the same 10,000 miles that our business used and 10,000 miles that our personal use required to equal 50% business use.

When I take the $15,000 of actual expenses times 50% business use my deduction just jumped to $7,500 on my schedule C line 9.

But I am not finished yet.

Let us pretend that I paid $30,000 for this vehicle and it is depreciated over a period of seven years. This is not perfect, but you are going to get the idea

I would take my $30,000 purchase price and divided by seven for a rough estimate of depreciation that would be about $4,285 a year , I multiply this by the 50% business use and that would give me an additional $2,143 deduction on my Schedule C line 13

Do you see the significant difference between these two different expense reporting options in this scenario?

In other situations, if you have low operating costs, you may be better served to do the flat mileage rate.

The only way you will know is to keep track of your business miles and your actual expenses.

There is a caveat here when you depreciate the vehicle and claim that deduction, you are going to sell the vehicle someday, depending upon the price that you sell the vehicle for, you may have a gain that must be brought back into the taxable income calculations on schedule C

Chances are that you will be replacing the old vehicle with a new one and a new depreciation schedule. Claiming depreciation on your old vehicle may not have any significant negative impact in the year of sale upon the purchase of a new vehicle.

I have oversimplified this discussion, but you should be able to get the idea of why it is important to compare both methods when you have a vehicle that has both personal and business use

In the next chapter we discuss what happens when you pay someone commissions in your business. In the following chapters we will be discussing many lines one by one with the next discussion point being line 10.

CHAPTER 16

Schedule C, line 10

Line 10- Do you pay a commission to someone to help sell your products? (A copy of a W9 is included at the endo of this chapter for reference.)

Are you giving them a 1099 form each January for the prior year monies you remitted to them?

I want you to look at the Schedule C starting at the top and refer to lines I & J about this line item.

If you pay anyone commissions, I encourage you to obtain a W9 form to gather their tax data to use for reference when the 1099 forms are completed and mailed in January of each year.

Failure to issue 1099's could cost you the deduction in an audit. Which will raise your taxes due, add penalties and interest on the adjustment.

It is less expensive than penalties for not submitting required tax forms, or to experience the deductions taken away when your time and money is involved to just file the 1099's each January as a matter of managing your ongoing business responsibilities.

I always get asked *"How much do I need to pay them each year, so I do not have to give them a 1099?"*

The easy answer is $600. The laws are always changing, and I would verify this figure annually.

I suggest you obtain a W9 for every person you pay commissions to, and issue 1099's to everyone each January. Then, you do not need to determine who gets one and who does not to minimize errors.

In the next chapter we discuss what happens when you pay someone contract wages in your business on line 11.

Form **W-9** (Rev. October 2018) Department of the Treasury Internal Revenue Service	**Request for Taxpayer Identification Number and Certification** ▶ Go to *www.irs.gov/FormW9* for instructions and the latest information.	Give Form to the requester. Do not send to the IRS.

<table>
<tr><td rowspan="9" style="writing-mode:vertical">Print or type.
See Specific Instructions on page 3.</td><td colspan="2">1 Name (as shown on your income tax return). Name is required on this line; do not leave this line blank.</td></tr>
<tr><td colspan="2">2 Business name/disregarded entity name, if different from above</td></tr>
<tr><td>3 Check appropriate box for federal tax classification of the person whose name is entered on line 1. Check only **one** of the following seven boxes.

☐ Individual/sole proprietor or single-member LLC   ☐ C Corporation   ☐ S Corporation   ☐ Partnership   ☐ Trust/estate

☐ Limited liability company. Enter the tax classification (C=C corporation, S=S corporation, P=Partnership) ▶ _____

Note: Check the appropriate box in the line above for the tax classification of the single-member owner. Do not check LLC if the LLC is classified as a single-member LLC that is disregarded from the owner unless the owner of the LLC is another LLC that is **not** disregarded from the owner for U.S. federal tax purposes. Otherwise, a single-member LLC that is disregarded from the owner should check the appropriate box for the tax classification of its owner.

☐ Other (see instructions) ▶</td><td>4 Exemptions (codes apply only to certain entities, not individuals; see instructions on page 3):

Exempt payee code (if any) _____

Exemption from FATCA reporting code (if any) _____

(Applies to accounts maintained outside the U.S.)</td></tr>
<tr><td colspan="2">5 Address (number, street, and apt. or suite no.) See instructions.   Requester's name and address (optional)</td></tr>
<tr><td colspan="2">6 City, state, and ZIP code</td></tr>
<tr><td colspan="2">7 List account number(s) here (optional)</td></tr>
</table>

Part I	**Taxpayer Identification Number (TIN)**

Enter your TIN in the appropriate box. The TIN provided must match the name given on line 1 to avoid backup withholding. For individuals, this is generally your social security number (SSN). However, for a resident alien, sole proprietor, or disregarded entity, see the instructions for Part I, later. For other entities, it is your employer identification number (EIN). If you do not have a number, see *How to get a TIN*, later.

Note: If the account is in more than one name, see the instructions for line 1. Also see *What Name and Number To Give the Requester* for guidelines on whose number to enter.

Social security number

☐☐☐ – ☐☐ – ☐☐☐☐

or

Employer identification number

☐☐ – ☐☐☐☐☐☐☐

Part II	**Certification**

Under penalties of perjury, I certify that:

1. The number shown on this form is my correct taxpayer identification number (or I am waiting for a number to be issued to me); and
2. I am not subject to backup withholding because: (a) I am exempt from backup withholding, or (b) I have not been notified by the Internal Revenue Service (IRS) that I am subject to backup withholding as a result of a failure to report all interest or dividends, or (c) the IRS has notified me that I am no longer subject to backup withholding; and
3. I am a U.S. citizen or other U.S. person (defined below); and
4. The FATCA code(s) entered on this form (if any) indicating that I am exempt from FATCA reporting is correct.

Certification instructions. You must cross out item 2 above if you have been notified by the IRS that you are currently subject to backup withholding because you have failed to report all interest and dividends on your tax return. For real estate transactions, item 2 does not apply. For mortgage interest paid, acquisition or abandonment of secured property, cancellation of debt, contributions to an individual retirement arrangement (IRA), and generally, payments other than interest and dividends, you are not required to sign the certification, but you must provide your correct TIN. See the instructions for Part II, later.

Sign Here	Signature of U.S. person ▶ Date ▶

General Instructions

Section references are to the Internal Revenue Code unless otherwise noted.

Future developments. For the latest information about developments related to Form W-9 and its instructions, such as legislation enacted after they were published, go to *www.irs.gov/FormW9*.

Purpose of Form

An individual or entity (Form W-9 requester) who is required to file an information return with the IRS must obtain your correct taxpayer identification number (TIN) which may be your social security number (SSN), individual taxpayer identification number (ITIN), adoption taxpayer identification number (ATIN), or employer identification number (EIN), to report on an information return the amount paid to you, or other amount reportable on an information return. Examples of information returns include, but are not limited to, the following.

• Form 1099-INT (interest earned or paid)

• Form 1099-DIV (dividends, including those from stocks or mutual funds)

• Form 1099-MISC (various types of income, prizes, awards, or gross proceeds)

• Form 1099-B (stock or mutual fund sales and certain other transactions by brokers)

• Form 1099-S (proceeds from real estate transactions)

• Form 1099-K (merchant card and third party network transactions)

• Form 1098 (home mortgage interest), 1098-E (student loan interest), 1098-T (tuition)

• Form 1099-C (canceled debt)

• Form 1099-A (acquisition or abandonment of secured property)

Use Form W-9 only if you are a U.S. person (including a resident alien), to provide your correct TIN.

If you do not return Form W-9 to the requester with a TIN, you might be subject to backup withholding. See What is backup withholding, later.

MONEY WITH AMY SERIES

SELF-EMPLOYED TAXES:
Unleashing Schedule C Deductions

Line 11 - Do you employ virtual assistants (VA's) or other non-W2 persons or entities to help you in your business? (A copy of a W9 is included at the end of this chapter for reference.)

Are you giving them a 1099 each January for the prior year monies you remitted to them?

I want you to look at the Schedule C starting at the top and refer to lines I & J about this line item.

If you pay anyone on a contract labor basis, I encourage you to obtain a W9 form to gather their tax data to use for reference when the 1099 forms are completed and mailed in January of each year.

Failure to issue 1099's could cost you the deduction in an audit. Which will raise your taxes due, add penalties and interest on the adjustment.

It is less expensive than penalties for not submitting required tax forms, or to experience the deductions taken away when your time and money is involved to just file the 1099's each January as a matter of managing your ongoing business responsibilities.

I always get asked *"How much do I need to pay them each year, so I do not have to give them a 1099?'*

The easy answer is $600. The laws are always changing, and I would verify this figure annually.

I suggest you obtain a W9 for every person or entity you pay contract amounts to, and issue 1099's to everyone each January. Then, you do not need to determine who gets one and who does not to minimize errors.

If you employ individual VA's or contractors that are foreign based, you do not need to issue them a US based 1099. You will need to have a form W-8BEN form on file though. (Copy of only page 1 of this form for reference included at the end of the chapter.)

If they are a foreign entity, you need form W-8BEN-E on file. (Copy of only page 1 this form for reference included at the end of the chapter.

In our next chapter we learn about depreciation on line 13.

Form W-9
(Rev. October 2018)
Department of the Treasury
Internal Revenue Service

Request for Taxpayer
Identification Number and Certification

▶ Go to www.irs.gov/FormW9 for instructions and the latest information.

Give Form to the requester. Do not send to the IRS.

Print or type.
See Specific Instructions on page 3.

1 Name (as shown on your income tax return). Name is required on this line; do not leave this line blank.

2 Business name/disregarded entity name, if different from above

3 Check appropriate box for federal tax classification of the person whose name is entered on line 1. Check only **one** of the following seven boxes.

☐ Individual/sole proprietor or single-member LLC   ☐ C Corporation   ☐ S Corporation   ☐ Partnership   ☐ Trust/estate

☐ Limited liability company. Enter the tax classification (C=C corporation, S=S corporation, P=Partnership) ▶ _____

Note: Check the appropriate box in the line above for the tax classification of the single-member owner. Do not check LLC if the LLC is classified as a single-member LLC that is disregarded from the owner unless the owner of the LLC is another LLC that is **not** disregarded from the owner for U.S. federal tax purposes. Otherwise, a single-member LLC that is disregarded from the owner should check the appropriate box for the tax classification of its owner.

☐ Other (see instructions) ▶

4 Exemptions (codes apply only to certain entities, not individuals; see instructions on page 3):

Exempt payee code (if any) _____

Exemption from FATCA reporting code (if any) _____

(Applies to accounts maintained outside the U.S.)

5 Address (number, street, and apt. or suite no.) See instructions.

6 City, state, and ZIP code

Requester's name and address (optional)

7 List account number(s) here (optional)

Part I   Taxpayer Identification Number (TIN)

Enter your TIN in the appropriate box. The TIN provided must match the name given on line 1 to avoid backup withholding. For individuals, this is generally your social security number (SSN). However, for a resident alien, sole proprietor, or disregarded entity, see the instructions for Part I, later. For other entities, it is your employer identification number (EIN). If you do not have a number, see *How to get a TIN*, later.

Note: If the account is in more than one name, see the instructions for line 1. Also see *What Name and Number To Give the Requester* for guidelines on whose number to enter.

Social security number

☐☐☐ – ☐☐ – ☐☐☐☐

or

Employer identification number

☐☐ – ☐☐☐☐☐☐☐

Part II   Certification

Under penalties of perjury, I certify that:

1. The number shown on this form is my correct taxpayer identification number (or I am waiting for a number to be issued to me); and
2. I am not subject to backup withholding because: (a) I am exempt from backup withholding, or (b) I have not been notified by the Internal Revenue Service (IRS) that I am subject to backup withholding as a result of a failure to report all interest or dividends, or (c) the IRS has notified me that I am no longer subject to backup withholding; and
3. I am a U.S. citizen or other U.S. person (defined below); and
4. The FATCA code(s) entered on this form (if any) indicating that I am exempt from FATCA reporting is correct.

Certification instructions. You must cross out item 2 above if you have been notified by the IRS that you are currently subject to backup withholding because you have failed to report all interest and dividends on your tax return. For real estate transactions, item 2 does not apply. For mortgage interest paid, acquisition or abandonment of secured property, cancellation of debt, contributions to an individual retirement arrangement (IRA), and generally, payments other than interest and dividends, you are not required to sign the certification, but you must provide your correct TIN. See the instructions for Part II, later.

Sign Here

Signature of U.S. person ▶   Date ▶

General Instructions

Section references are to the Internal Revenue Code unless otherwise noted.

Future developments. For the latest information about developments related to Form W-9 and its instructions, such as legislation enacted after they were published, go to www.irs.gov/FormW9.

Purpose of Form

An individual or entity (Form W-9 requester) who is required to file an information return with the IRS must obtain your correct taxpayer identification number (TIN) which may be your social security number (SSN), individual taxpayer identification number (ITIN), adoption taxpayer identification number (ATIN), or employer identification number (EIN), to report on an information return the amount paid to you, or other amount reportable on an information return. Examples of information returns include, but are not limited to, the following.

• Form 1099-INT (interest earned or paid)

• Form 1099-DIV (dividends, including those from stocks or mutual funds)

• Form 1099-MISC (various types of income, prizes, awards, or gross proceeds)

• Form 1099-B (stock or mutual fund sales and certain other transactions by brokers)

• Form 1099-S (proceeds from real estate transactions)

• Form 1099-K (merchant card and third party network transactions)

• Form 1098 (home mortgage interest), 1098-E (student loan interest), 1098-T (tuition)

• Form 1099-C (canceled debt)

• Form 1099-A (acquisition or abandonment of secured property)

Use Form W-9 only if you are a U.S. person (including a resident alien), to provide your correct TIN.

If you do not return Form W-9 to the requester with a TIN, you might be subject to backup withholding. See What is backup withholding, later.

Cat. No. 10231X   Form **W-9** (Rev. 10-2018)

79

Form W-8BEN

(Rev. October 2021)

Department of the Treasury
Internal Revenue Service

Certificate of Foreign Status of Beneficial Owner for United States Tax Withholding and Reporting (Individuals)

▶ For use by individuals. Entities must use Form W-8BEN-E.
▶ Go to *www.irs.gov/FormW8BEN* for instructions and the latest information.
▶ Give this form to the withholding agent or payer. Do not send to the IRS.

OMB No. 1545-1621

Do NOT use this form if:	Instead, use Form:
• You are NOT an individual	W-8BEN-E
• You are a U.S. citizen or other U.S. person, including a resident alien individual	W-9
• You are a beneficial owner claiming that income is effectively connected with the conduct of trade or business within the United States (other than personal services)	W-8ECI
• You are a beneficial owner who is receiving compensation for personal services performed in the United States	8233 or W-4
• You are a person acting as an intermediary	W-8IMY

Note: If you are resident in a FATCA partner jurisdiction (that is, a Model 1 IGA jurisdiction with reciprocity), certain tax account information may be provided to your jurisdiction of residence.

Part I Identification of Beneficial Owner (see instructions)

1 Name of individual who is the beneficial owner

2 Country of citizenship

3 Permanent residence address (street, apt. or suite no., or rural route). **Do not use a P.O. box or in-care-of address.**

City or town, state or province. Include postal code where appropriate.

Country

4 Mailing address (if different from above)

City or town, state or province. Include postal code where appropriate.

Country

5 U.S. taxpayer identification number (SSN or ITIN), if required (see instructions)

6a Foreign tax identifying number (see instructions)

6b Check if FTIN not legally required . . . . ☐

7 Reference number(s) (see instructions)

8 Date of birth (MM-DD-YYYY) (see instructions)

Part II Claim of Tax Treaty Benefits (for chapter 3 purposes only) (see instructions)

9 I certify that the beneficial owner is a resident of _____ within the meaning of the income tax treaty between the United States and that country.

10 **Special rates and conditions** (if applicable—see instructions): The beneficial owner is claiming the provisions of Article and paragraph _____ of the treaty identified on line 9 above to claim a _____ % rate of withholding on (specify type of income): _____.

Explain the additional conditions in the Article and paragraph the beneficial owner meets to be eligible for the rate of withholding:

Part III Certification

Under penalties of perjury, I declare that I have examined the information on this form and to the best of my knowledge and belief it is true, correct, and complete. I further certify under penalties of perjury that:

• I am the individual that is the beneficial owner (or am authorized to sign for the individual that is the beneficial owner) of all the income or proceeds to which this form relates or am using this form to document myself for chapter 4 purposes;

• The person named on line 1 of this form is not a U.S. person;

• This form relates to:

(a) income not effectively connected with the conduct of a trade or business in the United States;

(b) income effectively connected with the conduct of a trade or business in the United States but is not subject to tax under an applicable income tax treaty;

(c) the partner's share of a partnership's effectively connected taxable income; or

(d) the partner's amount realized from the transfer of a partnership interest subject to withholding under section 1446(f);

• The person named on line 1 of this form is a resident of the treaty country listed on line 9 of the form (if any) within the meaning of the income tax treaty between the United States and that country; and

• For broker transactions or barter exchanges, the beneficial owner is an exempt foreign person as defined in the instructions.

Furthermore, I authorize this form to be provided to any withholding agent that has control, receipt, or custody of the income of which I am the beneficial owner or any withholding agent that can disburse or make payments of the income of which I am the beneficial owner. **I agree that I will submit a new form within 30 days if any certification made on this form becomes incorrect.**

Sign Here ▶

☐ I certify that I have the capacity to sign for the person identified on line 1 of this form.

_____
Signature of beneficial owner (or individual authorized to sign for beneficial owner)

_____
Date (MM-DD-YYYY)

Print name of signer

For Paperwork Reduction Act Notice, see separate instructions.   Cat. No. 25047Z   Form **W-8BEN** (Rev. 10-2021)

Form **W-8BEN-E**

(Rev. October 2021)

Department of the Treasury
Internal Revenue Service

Certificate of Status of Beneficial Owner for United States Tax Withholding and Reporting (Entities)

▶ For use by entities. Individuals must use Form W-8BEN. ▶ Section references are to the Internal Revenue Code.
▶ Go to *www.irs.gov/FormW8BENE* for instructions and the latest information.
▶ Give this form to the withholding agent or payer. Do not send to the IRS.

OMB No. 1545-1621

Do NOT use this form for: **Instead use Form:**

- U.S. entity or U.S. citizen or resident W-9
- A foreign individual . . . . W-8BEN (Individual) or Form 8233
- A foreign individual or entity claiming that income is effectively connected with the conduct of trade or business within the United States (unless claiming treaty benefits) W-8ECI
- A foreign partnership, a foreign simple trust, or a foreign grantor trust (unless claiming treaty benefits) (see instructions for exceptions) . . . W-8IMY
- A foreign government, international organization, foreign central bank of issue, foreign tax-exempt organization, foreign private foundation, or government of a U.S. possession claiming that income is effectively connected U.S. income or that is claiming the applicability of section(s) 115(2), 501(c), 892, 895, or 1443(b) (unless claiming treaty benefits) (see instructions for other exceptions) . . . . W-8ECI or W-8EXP
- Any person acting as an intermediary (including a qualified intermediary acting as a qualified derivatives dealer) W-8IMY

| Part I | Identification of Beneficial Owner |

1 Name of organization that is the beneficial owner

2 Country of incorporation or organization

3 Name of disregarded entity receiving the payment (if applicable, see instructions)

4 Chapter 3 Status (entity type) (Must check one box only):

- ☐ Corporation
- ☐ Partnership
- ☐ Simple trust
- ☐ Tax-exempt organization
- ☐ Complex trust
- ☐ Foreign Government - Controlled Entity
- ☐ Central Bank of Issue
- ☐ Private foundation
- ☐ Estate
- ☐ Foreign Government - Integral Part
- ☐ Grantor trust
- ☐ Disregarded entity
- ☐ International organization

If you entered disregarded entity, partnership, simple trust, or grantor trust above, is the entity a hybrid making a treaty claim? If "Yes," complete Part III. ☐ Yes ☐ No

5 Chapter 4 Status (FATCA status) (See instructions for details and complete the certification below for the entity's applicable status.)

- ☐ Nonparticipating FFI (including an FFI related to a Reporting IGA FFI other than a deemed-compliant FFI, participating FFI, or exempt beneficial owner).
- ☐ Participating FFI.
- ☐ Reporting Model 1 FFI.
- ☐ Reporting Model 2 FFI.
- ☐ Registered deemed-compliant FFI (other than a reporting Model 1 FFI, sponsored FFI, or nonreporting IGA FFI covered in Part XII). See instructions.
- ☐ Sponsored FFI. Complete Part IV.
- ☐ Certified deemed-compliant nonregistering local bank. Complete Part V.
- ☐ Certified deemed-compliant FFI with only low-value accounts. Complete Part VI.
- ☐ Certified deemed-compliant sponsored, closely held investment vehicle. Complete Part VII.
- ☐ Certified deemed-compliant limited life debt investment entity. Complete Part VIII.
- ☐ Certain investment entities that do not maintain financial accounts. Complete Part IX.
- ☐ Owner-documented FFI. Complete Part X.
- ☐ Restricted distributor. Complete Part XI.

- ☐ Nonreporting IGA FFI. Complete Part XII.
- ☐ Foreign government, government of a U.S. possession, or foreign central bank of issue. Complete Part XIII.
- ☐ International organization. Complete Part XIV.
- ☐ Exempt retirement plans. Complete Part XV.
- ☐ Entity wholly owned by exempt beneficial owners. Complete Part XVI.
- ☐ Territory financial institution. Complete Part XVII.
- ☐ Excepted nonfinancial group entity. Complete Part XVIII.
- ☐ Excepted nonfinancial start-up company. Complete Part XIX.
- ☐ Excepted nonfinancial entity in liquidation or bankruptcy. Complete Part XX.
- ☐ 501(c) organization. Complete Part XXI.
- ☐ Nonprofit organization. Complete Part XXII.
- ☐ Publicly traded NFFE or NFFE affiliate of a publicly traded corporation. Complete Part XXIII.
- ☐ Excepted territory NFFE. Complete Part XXIV.
- ☐ Active NFFE. Complete Part XXV.
- ☐ Passive NFFE. Complete Part XXVI.
- ☐ Excepted inter-affiliate FFI. Complete Part XXVII.
- ☐ Direct reporting NFFE.
- ☐ Sponsored direct reporting NFFE. Complete Part XXVIII.
- ☐ Account that is not a financial account.

6 Permanent residence address (street, apt. or suite no., or rural route). **Do not use a P.O. box or in-care-of address** (other than a registered address).

City or town, state or province. Include postal code where appropriate.

Country

7 Mailing address (if different from above)

City or town, state or province. Include postal code where appropriate.

Country

For Paperwork Reduction Act Notice, see separate instructions.   Cat. No. 59689N   Form **W-8BEN-E** (Rev. 10-2021)

MONEY WITH AMY SERIES

SELF-EMPLOYED TAXES:
Unleashing Schedule C Deductions

Line 13-_Are you better off to take 100% depreciation within the special depreciation rules guidelines on your equipment including cell phone and computers, or spread it out over a period of tax years?

Are you depreciating your work vehicle in this line that holds hand with the information you place on line 9 we discussed above?

When you are in a high profit year, it may be most advantageous to depreciate eligible items in the tax year of purchase within guidelines.

In a low profit year when you expect your taxable income to rise in future tax years, you may be better served to stretch the deductions out over a period of years.

You will be able to choose by asset which method to apply.

You do not need to treat all depreciable assets with the same method on any given tax year. You have flexibility here.

I suggest you seek out qualified tax help on this one to know what is most advantageous for you year to year based on the most advantageous tax results over the life of the depreciable item.

In the next chapter we discuss employee benefit expenses and how employing a spouse in your Schedule C business may be advantageous to your household on line 14.

MONEY WITH AMY SERIES

SELF-EMPLOYED TAXES:
Unleashing Schedule C Deductions

Line 14- This one requires a discussion with a tax professional.

If you are married, should you employ your spouse and set up benefit packages using benefits in lieu of high wages that benefit your entire immediate family including you and your children?

Household dynamics vary too much for me to go into more detail here on how best to maximize the power of deductions from your taxable self-employment on line 14.

Add to the different dynamics or tax eligibility of the various plans, or changes in tax laws year to year, and it makes the need for a targeted discussion and correct handling of the recordkeeping on line 14 necessary.

Here is one you may not be familiar with: Have you heard of "De Minimis Fringe Benefits"?

Under the de minimis fringe benefit rules, your business deducts the cost of flowers, fruit, books, and comparable items given to you or your employees under special circumstances.

The recipients (both you and your employees) receive these fringe benefits tax-free, and the business deducts the expense. Talk to a professional about eligible items.

Do you see how my book you are reading right now to better manage your business taxation could be a potential deduction for helping you to structure your business accounting to reduce taxation?

What about implementing a medical reimbursement plan for non-covered out of pocket medical expenses for your family? Is this a clever idea for you?

Can you structure wages of a spouse or family members to create a benefit package to include paying for medical premiums that are not associated with any other outside W2 employer?

Now is the perfect time to have this important potential tax saving discussion with a tax professional!

In the next chapter we discuss the deductible business insurance topic on line 15.

MONEY WITH AMY SERIES

SELF-EMPLOYED TAXES:
Unleashing Schedule C Deductions

Line 15- Your casualty agent is an excellent resource here for designing the business-related coverage you may need.

Do you pay for professional liability insurance? Do you need it?

Should you be bonded?

Do you need to disclose to your homeowners or renters' insurance carrier that you have a home office on the premises and add a rider to the property coverage because you have clients meet you in your home office?

Do you have umbrella liability insurance because you want to have higher limits than your car, renters or homeowner's coverage provides because you have clients as passengers in your car or clients visiting your home office or home business-based location?

Talk to a tax professional on this point where you may need to add riders and split the premium costs in your policy for the portion that is deductible for the business and what is personal and non-deductible.

In our next chapter we talk about how to structure business interest to be deductible you may have missed on line 16b.

MONEY WITH AMY SERIES

SELF-EMPLOYED TAXES:
Unleashing Schedule C Deductions

Line 16b- I have clients who use revolving lines of credit, like credit cards, which are exclusively used for business expenses.

Are you deducting the interest you pay on these types of business purchases only cards?

Chances are you are deducting the purchases, but often neglecting to record the interest accrued on rolling credit card balances and that expense gets lost in your business expense recording.

This potential deduction has also been missed by taxpayers and preparers with the deferrals on loan accounts granted with the Covid19 calamity. The interest did not stop accruing on these loans, but the payments were suspended for a time.

There were also disaster related business loans that have been offered and accepted over the last several years that are accruing interest until paid off.

For a reference point, did you take out an EIDL or SBA loan or similar business loan during Covid or a disaster when offered? A record number of businesses accessed these offerings during tough times.

Are you deducting the interest portion paid annually on your EIDL or SBA loan? Did you even think about that?

I bet you have no idea where to get that interest and principal split information for EIDL or SBA.

You must print that information off the corresponding website that will tell you how much of your payment was interest, which is deductible, and the portion of the payments that was a reduction of principal.

Remember, repayment of principal is not a deductible expense.

What about any other disaster loans you may have taken over the years offered to you at trying times because of floods, wildfires and hurricanes or other natural disasters?

You would treat them in the same way as the EIDL loans when deducting the portion of the interest paid in the corresponding tax year.

In the next chapter we discuss potential legal and professional deductible expenses on line 17.

MONEY WITH AMY SERIES

SELF-EMPLOYED TAXES:
Unleashing Schedule C Deductions

Line 17 – There is a misconception here that 100% of your tax prep bill is a business expense. It is not from what I observe.

Why?

Not 100% of the data on your return is all Schedule C business related based on every tax return I have reviewed.

You do have other parts to your personal life that flow on the return too.

Here is an idea, you want to find out with that second or third opinion about your self-employment tax situation what you could do differently to your advantage. I believe that if the discussion is for the business, then the cost of those consults would be a business expense.

If you include in the discussion the potential tax consequences of selling your personal home and taking money out of a retirement account, that is personal advice.

In those cases, tell your professional you need to have the invoices split for tax purposes between personal and business-related topics.

Never muddy the expense records by combining personal expenses with business expenses. It will come back to bite you at some point.

Here is an idea for you. What if you engaged in a consultation with a business professional who was not located in your area and travel was required?

The cost of an engaging the business professional would still be a deductible expense 4for line 17.

In addition to that, your travel expenses, if structured and you keep records accurately, would potentially be a separate deductible expense on line 24a.

Do not let geography be a limiting factor to engage the professionals that you need to grow and manage your business.

In the next chapter we will talk about how the Schedule C proprietor can fund deposits into a retirement plan as the employer and deduct the expense saving Federal, State and Social Security taxes on the amount of the deposit recorded on the Schedule C line 19. With the right plan, the employee, who is the Schedule C proprietor, is not required to deposit personal dollars if they choose not to!

CHAPTER 23

Schedule C, line 19

Line 19- individuals using the schedule C play a dual role as taxpayers. The first role you play is as the employer. The second role you play is as the employee.

When you are operating in the dual role of employer (You on a Schedule C), you do have the option of matching the Employee (Also you on the Schedule C and 1040) eligible retirement plan contributions into plans such as Simple IRA's, 401k's, and Roth 401k's whether the Employee (you on the 1040) contribute to the plans or not.

Talk to a professional on this one and refer to the examples below for more insight on how this could work.

There are many different retirement plans tied to the business.

IRA and Roth IRAs are tied to W2 earnings and/or the net earnings of the business but are not tied directly to the business because they are personal retirement plans.

You can have both employer and personal retirement plan options in many situations based on the plan and income guidelines.

They say a picture is worth a thousand words.

Here are a series of quick illustrations for a sole proprietor to help you see how the contribution amounts can vary at different net Schedule C income levels for a self-employed professional.

Please note the illustrations show the maximum contributions. You could do less than these stated maximum contribution amounts, but not more.

If you really wanted to reposition assets into retirement accounts for estate, lawsuit, or other reasons, you could use a retirement plan that is tied to the business and max it out, then if eligible, max out allowable contributions to an IRA or Roth IRA too. How we arrange those entries on the tax return and how the tax dominoes fall will frame your options year to year.

It is important to note the Employer contribution will always be pre-tax deposits into the employee's accounts. The employer (you on the Schedule C) takes it as a deduction. The employee when it is withdrawn pays the tax on the contribution.

If you use a 401k plan, you have the flexibility as an Employee to put your contributions in either the pretax 401k or post tax into the 401k Roth, or a mixture of the two not to exceed guidelines.

With the clients I work with, we decide based on tax brackets what is the best short term and long-term contribution placement on a year-to-year basis.

Now let us review 5 different retirement funding possibility examples:

Example #1 Age 35 with a net profit of $65,000 a year

Notice the maximum amount the employer could contribute on behalf of the employee is $12,082? Even if the employee (you as a person) chooses not to add any money to the account, the employer can add $12,082 for this tax year example.

But does it really cost you $12,082? I say no.

Let us assume you are in a:

22% Federal income Tax Bracket
5% State Income Tax Bracket
15.3% Social Security Tax Bracket
42.3% combined tax rate potential savings on contributions eligible for Schedule C line 19

Your tax savings on a $12,082 eligible 401K employer retirement plan contribution on Schedule C line19 would be substantial.

Here is how we would estimate that tax savings. There could be tax savings, it depends on the tax ripple effect of each entry and whether you would change tax brackets in the process. Remember, every entry causes a tax domino effect somewhere.

For my calculations I am assuming that there is no other tax change to keep it simple.

$12,082 x 42.3%= $5,111 estimated tax savings

$12,082
-05,111
$6,971 net cost of the Employer 401K contribution

What if instead you put the same $12,082 personal contribution into a Simple IRA plan?

This is not eligible for the Schedule C line 19 tax treatment. It goes instead on the Schedule 1 line 16 tax return page that flows to the 1040 form.

We have a different tax result with this Simple IRA retirement plan contribution because we are only saving taxes on the Federal and state level when it is posted here on the return.

$12,082 x 27% = $3,262

$12,082
-03,262
$ 8,820 net cost of the Simple IRA contribution

This one decision in what retirement plan you select, and where a retirement contribution plan entry is placed on the return in this example using a Simple IRA increases a tax bill by $1,849!

Do you now understand that what type of plan you use and what line you put a contribution on the return makes a dramatic difference to how much of your earnings you get to keep?

Let me really blow your mind on this one.

What if you really wanted to load up the tax-free 401k Roth account instead of the taxable 401k plan?

Easy?

We let the employer, you the schedule C employer, put the contribution in the pre-tax 401k plan.

You, the employee, convert the pre-tax 401k to the tax-free Roth 401k and pay taxes on the $12,082 on a personal level. This would show up on the 1040-line 4a and 4b.

You still saved $1,849 by eliminating the Social Security taxes on the contribution deduction that went through the Schedule C!

At this point a couple of fair questions to ask you my reader would be:

> *Will your tax professional help you to arrange the entries that allow you to "keep" more of the money you earn by helping you structure your taxes to your advantage?*

> *How much has or will your tax preparer "cost" you when they prepare your taxes and do not tell you how to structure the entries to reduce your tax liability?*

Something to think about…

An Individual 401(k) allows for a $32,582 annual contribution for 2022.

This is based on an income of $65,000. For sole proprietors, this is the net income from your tax Schedule C or C-EZ. To calculate your maximum contribution, we assumed that you maximized all business contributions and elective deferrals. The table below summarizes Individual 401(k) contribution calculation along side SEP IRAs, SIMPLE IRAs and Profit Sharing plan contributions.

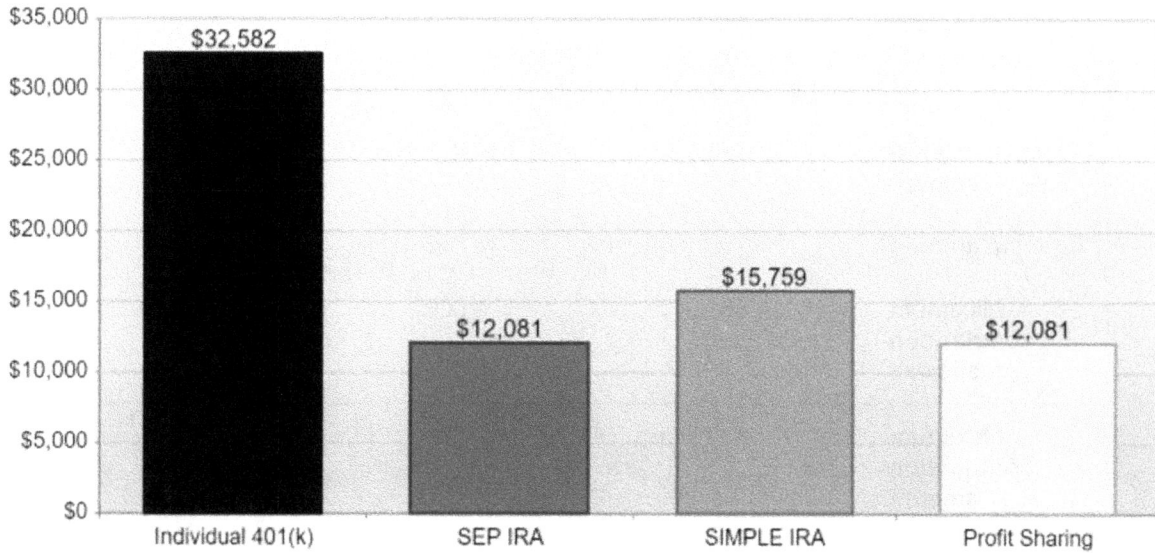

Individual 401(k)	SEP IRA	SIMPLE IRA	Profit Sharing
$32,582	$12,081	$15,759	$12,081

Input Summary	
Business type	Unincorporated Sole Proprietorship
Net income	$65,000
Current age	35

Results Summary				
	Individual 401(k) plan for 2022	SEP IRA for 2022	SIMPLE IRA for 2022	Profit Sharing plan for 2022
Adjusted earned income*	$48,326	$48,326	$58,648	$48,326
Employer contribution	$12,082 25% of Adjusted earned income	$12,081 25% of Adjusted earned income	$1,759 3% of Adjusted earned income	$12,081 25% of Adjusted earned income
Elective deferral amount	$20,500	NONE	$14,000	NONE
Catchup amount	$0	NONE	$0	NONE
Maximum contribution allowed	$61,000	$61,000	$28,000	$61,000
Maximum contribution amount	$32,582	$12,081	$15,759	$12,081

*Calculated as net business income of $65,000 - deduction for Self-Employment Tax of $4,592 divided by 1+ annual contribution percentage of the employer. This results in the total business profit after self employment taxes and employer contributions to the retirement plan. Maximum earned income allowed is $305,000.

Example #2 Age 45 with a net profit of $185,000 a year

An Individual 401(k) allows for a $55,182 annual contribution for 2022.

This is based on an income of $185,000. For sole proprietors, this is the net income from your tax Schedule C or C-EZ. To calculate your maximum contribution, we assumed that you maximized all business contributions and elective deferrals. The table below summarizes Individual 401(k) contribution calculation along side SEP IRAs, SIMPLE IRAs and Profit Sharing plan contributions.

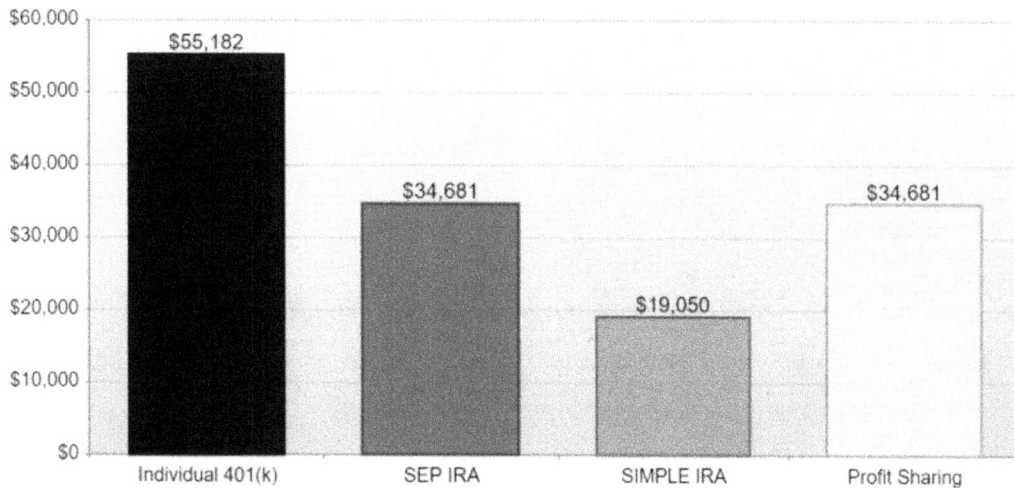

Input Summary	
Business type	Unincorporated Sole Proprietorship
Net income	$185,000
Current age	45

Results Summary				
	Individual 401(k) plan for 2022	SEP IRA for 2022	SIMPLE IRA for 2022	Profit Sharing plan for 2022
Adjusted earned income*	$138,727	$138,727	$168,358	$138,727
Employer contribution	$34,682 25% of Adjusted earned income	$34,681 25% of Adjusted earned income	$5,050 3% of Adjusted earned income	$34,681 25% of Adjusted earned income
Elective deferral amount	$20,500	NONE	$14,000	NONE
Catchup amount	$0	NONE	$0	NONE
Maximum contribution allowed	$61,000	$61,000	$28,000	$61,000
Maximum contribution amount	$55,182	$34,681	$19,050	$34,681

*Calculated as net business income of $185,000 - deduction for Self-Employment Tax of $11,591 divided by 1+ annual contribution percentage of the employer. This results in the total business profit after self employment taxes and employer contributions to the retirement plan. Maximum earned income allowed is $305,000.

<u>Example #3 Age 55 with a net profit of $265,000 a year</u>

An Individual 401(k) allows for a $67,500 annual contribution for 2022.

This is based on an income of $265,000. For sole proprietors, this is the net income from your tax Schedule C or C-EZ. To calculate your maximum contribution, we assumed that you maximized all business contributions and elective deferrals. The table below summarizes Individual 401(k) contribution calculation along side SEP IRAs, SIMPLE IRAs and Profit Sharing plan contributions.

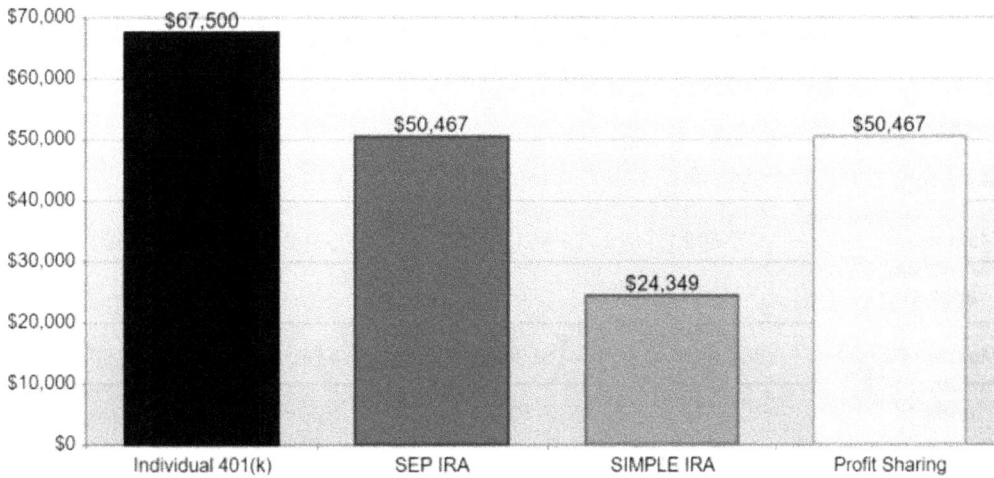

Input Summary	
Business type	Unincorporated Sole Proprietorship
Net income	$265,000
Current age	55

Results Summary				
	Individual 401(k) plan for 2022	SEP IRA for 2022	SIMPLE IRA for 2022	Profit Sharing plan for 2022
Adjusted earned income*	$201,869	$201,870	$244,988	$201,870
Employer contribution	$40,500 25% of Adjusted earned income	$50,467 25% of Adjusted earned income	$7,349 3% of Adjusted earned income	$50,467 25% of Adjusted earned income
Elective deferral amount	$20,500	NONE	$14,000	NONE
Catchup amount	$6,500	NONE	$3,000	NONE
Maximum contribution allowed	$67,500	$61,000	$31,000	$61,000
Maximum contribution amount	$67,500	$50,467	$24,349	$50,467

*Calculated as net business income of $265,000 - deduction for Self-Employment Tax of $12,663 divided by 1+ annual contribution percentage of the employer. This results in the total business profit after self employment taxes and employer contributions to the retirement plan. Maximum earned income allowed is $305,000.

Example #4 Age 65 with a net profit of $147,000 a year

Print   **Hide Report**

An Individual 401(k) allows for a $54,323 annual contribution for 2022.

This is based on an income of $147,000. For sole proprietors, this is the net income from your tax Schedule C or C-EZ. To calculate your maximum contribution, we assumed that you maximized all business contributions and elective deferrals. The table below summarizes Individual 401(k) contribution calculation along side SEP IRAs, SIMPLE IRAs and Profit Sharing plan contributions.

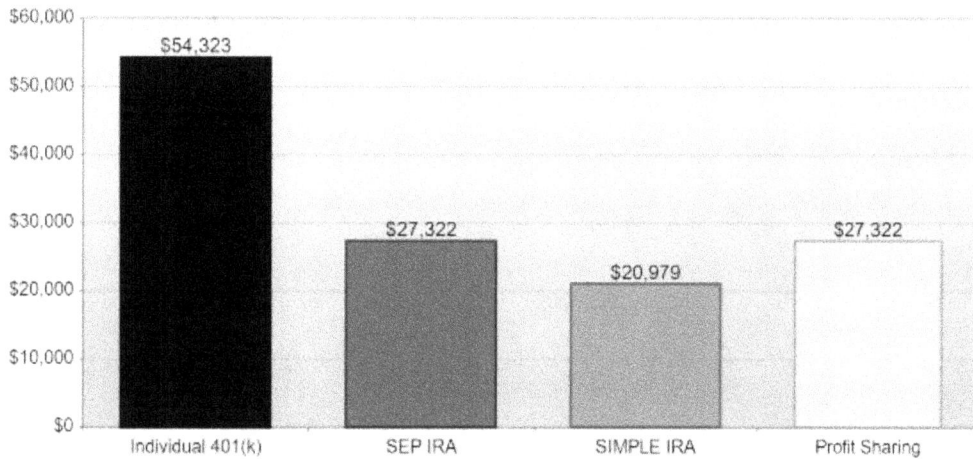

Input Summary	
Business type	Unincorporated Sole Proprietorship
Net income	$147,000
Current age	65

Results Summary				
	Individual 401(k) plan for 2022	SEP IRA for 2022	SIMPLE IRA for 2022	Profit Sharing plan for 2022
Adjusted earned income*	$109,292	$109,292	$132,636	$109,292
Employer contribution	$27,323 25% of Adjusted earned income	$27,322 25% of Adjusted earned income	$3,979 3% of Adjusted earned income	$27,322 25% of Adjusted earned income
Elective deferral amount	$20,500	NONE	$14,000	NONE
Catchup amount	$6,500	NONE	$3,000	NONE
Maximum contribution allowed	$67,500	$61,000	$31,000	$61,000
Maximum contribution amount	$54,323	$27,322	$20,979	$27,322

*Calculated as net business income of $147,000 - deduction for Self-Employment Tax of $10,385 divided by 1+ annual contribution percentage of the employer. This results in the total business profit after self employment taxes and employer contributions to the retirement plan. Maximum earned income allowed is $305,000

<u>Example #5 Age 75 with a net profit of $200,000 a year</u>

An Individual 401(k) allows for a $64,642 annual contribution for 2022.

This is based on an income of $200,000. For sole proprietors, this is the net income from your tax Schedule C or C-EZ. To calculate your maximum contribution, we assumed that you maximized all business contributions and elective deferrals. The table below summarizes Individual 401(k) contribution calculation along side SEP IRAs, SIMPLE IRAs and Profit Sharing plan contributions.

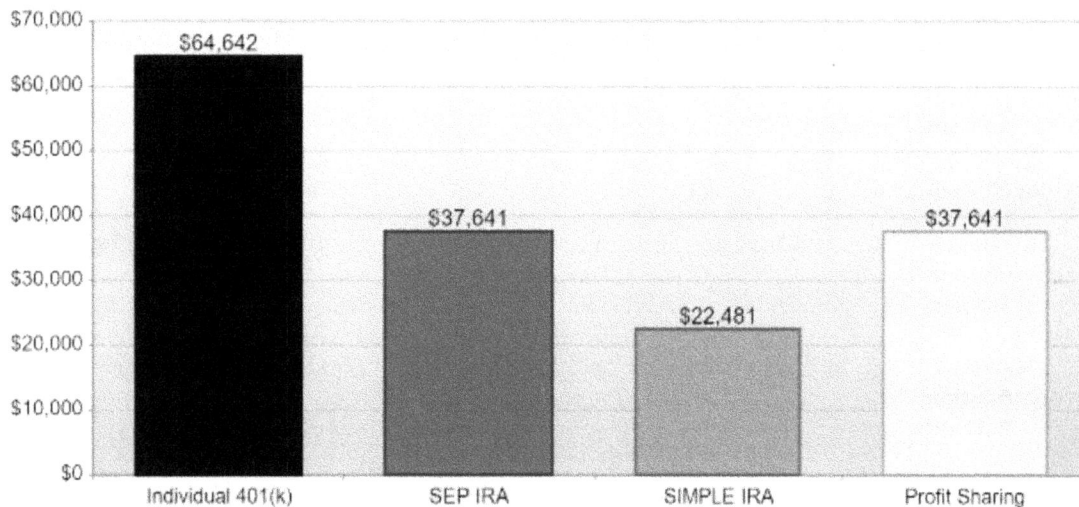

Input Summary	
Business type	Unincorporated Sole Proprietorship
Net income	$200,000
Current age	75

Results Summary				
	Individual 401(k) plan for 2022	SEP IRA for 2022	SIMPLE IRA for 2022	Profit Sharing plan for 2022
Adjusted earned income*	$150,566	$150,566	$182,726	$150,566
Employer contribution	$37,642 25% of Adjusted earned income	$37,641 25% of Adjusted earned income	$5,481 3% of Adjusted earned income	$37,641 25% of Adjusted earned income
Elective deferral amount	$20,500	NONE	$14,000	NONE
Catchup amount	$6,500	NONE	$3,000	NONE
Maximum contribution allowed	$67,500	$61,000	$31,000	$61,000
Maximum contribution amount	$64,642	$37,641	$22,481	$37,641

*Calculated as net business income of $200,000 - deduction for Self-Employment Tax of $11,792 divided by 1+ annual contribution percentage of the employer. This results in the total business profit after self employment taxes and employer contributions to the retirement plan. Maximum earned income allowed is $305,000.

In our next chapter we will touch on whether you can rent your home office or home business space from your spouse when they ow the property and you do not on line 20b.

MONEY WITH AMY SERIES

SELF-EMPLOYED TAXES:
Unleashing Schedule C Deductions

20b- If you do not own the property where your home office is located because your spouse is the property owner, you may be best served to rent space from your spouse.

It is more advantageous in most cases for you to deduct the expenses on your Schedule C saving Social Security taxes and for them to record the income and take the eligible rental deductions on Schedule E. The income will be subject to Federal and state income taxes either way, less any schedule E allowable deductions.

If you do not own the property and your spouse does, another angle may be to reimburse them for a percentage of the home expenses as it relates to the home-based office. I would use form 8829 discussed later in this book as a good guideline for reimbursements.

In a reimbursement situation, the Schedule C filer deducts the reimbursement on line 20, but because it is a reimbursement, the spouse who owns the property does not need to claim it as income as a reimbursement anywhere on the return.

Semantics and structure matter in these arrangements.

You choose the method best for you after comparing the two different results.

Yes, this is another area to discuss with a tax professional on how best to manage this type of situation.

Now is a suitable time to discuss deductible travel expenses on line 24a.

MONEY WITH AMY SERIES

SELF-EMPLOYED TAXES:
Unleashing Schedule C Deductions

24a- I know most business owners understand that when you go to a conference overnight or for the weekend in another city for a training seminar, the costs are deductible.

If you travel to a destination within the United States for business purposes, and you spend the guideline amounts of your trip days on business, you deduct 100 percent of your direct-route transportation expenses.

You may deduct meals and lodging for business days as well.

But…do you know how you could even write off a 4–7-day business related Caribbean cruise without batting an eye? Want to go on four a year? Ok.

How about a stay at a lovely resort?

Have I grabbed your attention?

I know how to do this. Do you?

It is possible to deduct longer business cruises too with the correct structuring. This one revelation alone must be worth giving me a call for help if your attention was captured on this opportunity.

Foreign travel expenses when you travel outside of the United States for business purposes for fewer than seven days have basic special rules you should be aware of.

You may deduct 100 percent of your transportation costs of getting to and from your foreign business destination — even if you work there only one day.

You may deduct meals and lodging for business days as well.

Did you ever think of this one?

Do you need training or want to attend a conference in another city? Structure it correctly and the travel costs are deductible.

If you went out of town to meet with your business advisor those expenses could be deductible too.

This is tax pro discussion material for certain.

Hint, hint…Think about how coming to spend time with me in person or on a cruise in lieu of a Zoom to get the one-on-one professional help you know you need could be another potential deductible trip for you.

Next it is time to learn about line 24b about deductible business meals.

MONEY WITH AMY SERIES

SELF-EMPLOYED TAXES:
Unleashing Schedule C Deductions

Line 24b – The rules over the last few years on deductible meals have been changing, mostly due to special Covid19 provisions. It is important to understand what is and what is not a business meal.

A business meal refers to a meal that is primarily conducted for business purposes, where the cost of the food and beverages consumed during the meal may be tax-deductible for businesses under certain conditions.

The definition of a business meal and what qualifies as a business meal may vary depending on the context and specific regulations.

Here is a comprehensive explanation of what is considered a business meal and what is not:

Business Meal:

A meal where a business owner or an employee of the business is present when food or beverages are provided.

The meal must be purchased from a restaurant, which includes establishments that prepare and sell food or beverages for immediate consumption by retail customers, both on-premises or off-premises.

The payment or billing for the food and beverages should occur in the tax year paid.

The expense should not be lavish or extravagant.

The cost of the meal can include taxes and tips.

Non-Qualifying Business Meal:

Meals purchased from grocery stores, convenience stores, and other businesses that primarily sell pre-packaged goods not intended for immediate consumption do not qualify as business meals.

Certain employer-operated eating facilities, including cafeterias or eating facilities located on business premises for employee meals, do not qualify as restaurants for the purpose of the enhanced meal deduction.

In summary, a business meal is a meal conducted for business purposes, where the cost of food and beverages purchased from a restaurant can be fully deducted for tax purposes under specific conditions.

Meals purchased from grocery stores or employer-operated eating facilities typically do not qualify as business meals.

It is important to consult the relevant tax laws and regulations or seek professional advice for specific details and requirements related to business meal deductions because they can and do change on deductible percentages from year to year from a low of 50% to a high of 100%.

In the next chapter we will touch on utilities expenses on line 25.

CHAPTER 27

Schedule C, line 25

MONEY WITH AMY SERIES

SELF-EMPLOYED TAXES:
Unleashing Schedule C Deductions

Line 25

This line item is best served with a discussion with your tax professional.

Why?

This potential deduction needs to be coordinated with other business operational relevant facts related to deciding factors such as:

Do you rent outside storage space that has separate utilities?

Do you claim a home office where these expenses will already be deducted as a percentage of the property operating costs on form 8829?

Let me show you an example of why this can result in complex calculations and require extra documentation in the file records at times.

The married taxpayer's own their home.

All utilities are shared with no separate meters.

They rent out an apartment on the premises that comprises 20% of the property.

Spouse #1 has a home office that comprises 21% of the property.

Spouse #1 has a home-based business that comprises 18% of the property.

The electric, gas, water, pest extermination, cable, internet, one land line, alarm system and trash bills paid total $14,330 in the tax year. The costs will be split out on the return as follows:

Personal portion of utilities will not be deducted anywhere on the return.

Apartment portion on Schedule E will be $14,330 x 20% = $2,866 deduction

Form 8829 for Spouse #1 entry will be $14,330 x 21% = $3,009 deduction

Form 8829 for Spouse #s entry will be $14,330 x 18% = $2,579 deduction

Does this example make sense to you? Do you see how important it is to have guidance to secure all the deductions you are entitled to and to record them correctly at the same time?

In the next chapter we discuss employing a spouse or minor aged children possibilities using W2 wages for line 26.

MONEY WITH AMY SERIES

SELF-EMPLOYED TAXES:
Unleashing Schedule C Deductions

Line 26- This is where you want to discuss employing your spouse if applicable with a tax professional. To be clear, they must work in the business. This means they do something related to operating your business.

There are also advantages to employing minor aged children to work in your business on a reasonable basis. To be clear, they must work in the business. This means they do something related to operating your business.

For an example, let us say you pay your intelligent 16-year-old daughter to help you stuff mailers monthly, drop off and mail items at the post office on demand and she helps you manage your accounts on Social Media. You pay her $10,000 a year to do these specific tasks.

There are additional monthly, quarterly, and annual responsibilities for having anyone in your Schedule C business to be on a W2 payroll. Talk to your tax professional for help before you do anything here!

You report these wages on a W2, and you fill in your related employer tax reporting forms in January of each year.

She will keep all $10,000, less any payroll deductions, of the income, tax free, because that is under her standard deduction for filing income taxes. She is to use the money to help pay for her clothing, operating a car expenses, her piano lessons and other things you agree upon.

She starts funding a tax-free Roth IRA too because she has wages in her own name.

She is under 18 so you can elect to not pay into her Social Security or unemployment insurance as a minor child.

You are in a combined Federal, State and Social Security tax bracket of 42.3%.

In this case paying her $10,000 a year for legitimate help in your business saves you $4,230 in taxes.

Employing your capable children may be something to consider in the right circumstances as a part of an overall tax reduction strategy.

When employing a spouse, you may choose to have nominal wages and fabulous benefits that help the entire household, you the Schedule C business owner included. In these cases where you employ a spouse, the deductions on the Schedule C lines 14 and 26 will hold hands and work together.

In the next chapter we move on to the miscellaneous expenses that really do not fit on the Schedule C lines 8-26 and fall on line 27a.

Line 27a is related to page 2 of the Schedule C Part V.

I have seen all kinds of business expenses here that are unique to the business, but they do not exactly match any of the categories on lines 8 through 26.

I do suggest my clients think in broad terms and try to make them fit in those lines and to minimize the amount of expenses that we put here.

There is no magic number that I am aware of that would cause an automatic flag for an audit on a return, but a good guideline that I like to use is no more than 10% of your overall expenses to fall into this category.

When they are all listed then the total that is online 48 will then flow to line 27a.
Now let me tell you one unusual expense example that I found to be a necessary business expense for the structure of Comedian Gallagher's business model I heard about years ago. I suppose it could fall under supplies too.

Comedian Gallagher was known for deducting watermelons as a business expense related to his performances. He became famous for his prop comedy routine, which included his signature act of smashing watermelons on stage with a wooden sledgehammer known as the "Sledge-O-Matic" .

The act of smashing watermelons was part of Gallagher's comedic gimmick, and he saw it as an unforgettable way to entertain and bring excitement to his shows. The watermelon-smashing routine became one of his trademark acts, and he performed it extensively during his career, destroying tens of thousands of melons with the Sledge-O-Matic.

While Gallagher's watermelon-smashing act may have been an integral part of his comedy routine, it is important to note that the deductibility of watermelons as a business expense would depend on the specific circumstances and whether they were related to his trade or business.

Deductions for business expenses require meeting certain criteria and substantiation, and the specifics of Gallagher's tax deductions would be based on his individual tax filings and the guidance provided by the IRS.

So, what could go in this section for the operations of your business may or may not include a Sledge-O-Matic or watermelons!

In the next chapter we will briefly touch on line 30 as it relates to your home office.

CHAPTER 30

Schedule C, line 30

Line 30- Do you operate your business out of your home?

Then you need to be familiar with form 8829 and how to set up a home office or workshop to meet the eligibility guidelines.

Whether you choose to do actual expenses or take a flat amount per square foot, this is a deduction that needs to be maximized.

Form 8829 (A copy of the form is inserted at the end of this chapter for reference.)

When you are self-employed, this form allows you to deduct either a flat amount per square foot up to guideline limits or your actual expenses by a percentage of your home.

If you are a homeowner, any percentage of home loan interest and taxes that are taken here on form 8829 against self-employment income will reduce the deductions dollar for dollar for these items on your Schedule A, if you are able to itemize.

If you are not able to itemize, this is a huge win. You are converting previously non-deductible home operating expenses of home interest and real estate taxes that do absolutely nothing for you on Schedule A to deductible ones on the form 8829.

For homeowners, using form 8829 allows you to include the applicable percentage of non-deductible expenses including repairs, maintenance, HOA fees, utilities, and insurance! A huge win to reduce your Federal, state and Social Security taxes!

If you are a renter, you still benefit by being able to deduct a percentage of rent, utilities, and any repairs you do to the unit that you could not deduct before on any form.

To get a grasp of how important this could be to you, let us discuss hypothetical examples.

Example of how form 8829 reduces your tax liability

Homeowner/self-employed person cannot itemize on Schedule A.

Total eligible home office expenses on form 8829 total $35,000.

The home was purchased last year for $250,000.

25% of the home is used for business.

On Schedule C, the self-employed business owner had a tentative profit on Schedule C line 29 of $110,000.

The self-employed person is in the following tax brackets:
Federal 22%
State 5%

Social Security 15.3%

Before the home office deduction, the self-employed person would be liable for the following taxes:

Federal	$24,200
State	+ 5,500
Social Security	+16,830
Total taxes on $100k tentative profits	$46,530

With correctly structuring the home office deductions the taxpayer realizes the following deduction on form 8829 that flows to the Schedule C line 30.

Allowable operating expenses	-$ 8,750
Allowable home depreciation	- 2,232
Total deduction on line 30	- $10,892

New net taxable income is $110,000 – 10,892 = $99,108

Tax bills due reduce to:

Federal	$21,804
State	+ 4,955
Social Security	+15,163
Total taxes on $99,108 tentative profits	$41,922

Tax savings in this example $46,530-41,922 = $4,608.

Is there another option for a home office deduction?

Yes, and you can choose to use the one that gives you the highest deduction, or not.

What if you do not want to bother keeping track of all those operating expenses for another deduction?

Then you may want to take the flat deduction.

For the same taxpayer circumstances above, assuming the Home Office was at least 300 square feet of the home, they are entitled to take a flat $5 per square foot deduction.

300 square feet times $5 per square feet equals a maximum $1,500 deduction on the Schedule C line 30.

The tax savings on a $1,500 deduction for the same taxpayer would only be $635.

The taxpayer has the choice, based on recordkeeping, whether they want to experience a $4,608 or $635 reduction in tax liabilities by claiming the home office.

I am certain I know which option I would be taking!

What about you? Do you have a preference?

By here, you should be able to grasp how with careful structuring, you can dramatically reduce your tax liability in multiple areas that collectively add up to a substantial reduction in overall tax liabilities.

This is how you keep more of what you earn by giving away less to taxes you should not owe.

Tax reduction does not happen by chance.

The good news is that you get to choose whether you want to do less recordkeeping and pay more in taxes or do a little more structuring and annual planning to pay less income taxes.

Just claiming a home office may be to your advantage that could have a bottom-line positive influence of tens or hundreds of thousands of dollars less in taxes over your tax paying lifetime.

In our next chapter, we visit about the Earned Income Credit (EIC) windfall that could be an unexpected refund gift on a tax year where you have truly little taxable income because of the way the numbers fell on the paper from form EIC.

Form **8829**

Department of the Treasury
Internal Revenue Service

Expenses for Business Use of Your Home

File only with Schedule C (Form 1040). Use a separate Form 8829 for each home you used for business during the year.
Go to *www.irs.gov/Form8829* for instructions and the latest information.

OMB No. 1545-0074

2022

Attachment
Sequence No. **176**

Name(s) of proprietor(s)

Your social security number

Part I Part of Your Home Used for Business

1	Area used regularly and exclusively for business, regularly for daycare, or for storage of inventory or product samples (see instructions)	**1**	
2	Total area of home	**2**	
3	Divide line 1 by line 2. Enter the result as a percentage	**3**	%
	For daycare facilities not used exclusively for business, go to line 4. All others, go to line 7.		
4	Multiply days used for daycare during year by hours used per day · · · **4** hr.		
5	If you started or stopped using your home for daycare during the year, see instructions; otherwise, enter 8,760 · · · · · · · **5** hr.		
6	Divide line 4 by line 5. Enter the result as a decimal amount · · · · **6**		
7	Business percentage. For daycare facilities not used exclusively for business, multiply line 6 by line 3 (enter the result as a percentage). All others, enter the amount from line 3 · · · · · ·	**7**	%

Part II Figure Your Allowable Deduction

8	Enter the amount from Schedule C, line 29, **plus** any gain derived from the business use of your home, **minus** any loss from the trade or business not derived from the business use of your home. See instructions.	**8**	

See instructions for columns (a) and (b) before completing lines 9–22.

			(a) Direct expenses	(b) Indirect expenses	
9	Casualty losses (see instructions)	**9**			
10	Deductible mortgage interest (see instructions)	**10**			
11	Real estate taxes (see instructions)	**11**			
12	Add lines 9, 10, and 11	**12**			
13	Multiply line 12, column (b), by line 7		**13**		
14	Add line 12, column (a), and line 13				**14**
15	Subtract line 14 from line 8. If zero or less, enter -0-				**15**
16	Excess mortgage interest (see instructions)	**16**			
17	Excess real estate taxes (see instructions)	**17**			
18	Insurance	**18**			
19	Rent	**19**			
20	Repairs and maintenance	**20**			
21	Utilities	**21**			
22	Other expenses (see instructions)	**22**			
23	Add lines 16 through 22	**23**			
24	Multiply line 23, column (b), by line 7		**24**		
25	Carryover of prior year operating expenses (see instructions)		**25**		
26	Add line 23, column (a), line 24, and line 25				**26**
27	Allowable operating expenses. Enter the **smaller** of line 15 or line 26				**27**
28	Limit on excess casualty losses and depreciation. Subtract line 27 from line 15				**28**
29	Excess casualty losses (see instructions)		**29**		
30	Depreciation of your home from line 42 below		**30**		
31	Carryover of prior year excess casualty losses and depreciation (see instructions)		**31**		
32	Add lines 29 through 31				**32**
33	Allowable excess casualty losses and depreciation. Enter the **smaller** of line 28 or line 32				**33**
34	Add lines 14, 27, and 33				**34**
35	Casualty loss portion, if any, from lines 14 and 33. Carry amount to **Form 4684.** See instructions				**35**
36	**Allowable expenses for business use of your home.** Subtract line 35 from line 34. Enter here and on Schedule C, line 30. If your home was used for more than one business, see instructions				**36**

Part III Depreciation of Your Home

37	Enter the **smaller** of your home's adjusted basis or its fair market value. See instructions	**37**	
38	Value of land included on line 37	**38**	
39	Basis of building. Subtract line 38 from line 37	**39**	
40	Business basis of building. Multiply line 39 by line 7	**40**	
41	Depreciation percentage (see instructions)	**41**	%
42	Depreciation allowable (see instructions). Multiply line 40 by line 41. Enter here and on line 30 above	**42**	

Part IV Carryover of Unallowed Expenses to 2023

43	Operating expenses. Subtract line 27 from line 26. If less than zero, enter -0-	**43**	
44	Excess casualty losses and depreciation. Subtract line 33 from line 32. If less than zero, enter -0-.	**44**	

For Paperwork Reduction Act Notice, see your tax return instructions.   Cat. No. 13232M   Form **8829** (2022)

123

CHAPTER 31

Schedule EIC

MONEY WITH AMY SERIES

SELF-EMPLOYED TAXES:
Unleashing Schedule C Deductions

<u>Schedule EIC</u> (A copy of the form is inserted at the end of this chapter for reference.)

Form EIC will only apply if your income meets the eligibility guidelines.

I mentioned above that I have seen this tax credit happen as a surprise one-time occurrence in a year with large losses and transitions into entrepreneurship that deflate income in a single tax year.

When all those tax dominoes I mentioned above fall in a specific net taxable income level sequence, this tax credit is triggered for taxpayers who have never received it before, it is a gift.

I tell my clients never count on this refund ever happening to you again.

Why?

Circumstances, your taxable income, and tax laws change. Here today could easily be gone tomorrow for this windfall.

SCHEDULE EIC
(Form 1040)

Department of the Treasury
Internal Revenue Service

Earned Income Credit

Qualifying Child Information

Complete and attach to Form 1040 or 1040-SR only if you have a qualifying child.
Go to *www.irs.gov/ScheduleEIC* for the latest information.

OMB No. 1545-0074

2022

Attachment
Sequence No. **43**

Name(s) shown on return

Your social security number

If you are separated from your spouse, filing a separate return, and meet the requirements to claim the EIC (see instructions), check here ☐

Before you begin:
- See the instructions for Form 1040, line 27, to make sure that (a) you can take the EIC, and (b) you have a qualifying child.
- Be sure the child's name on line 1 and social security number (SSN) on line 2 agree with the child's social security card. Otherwise, at the time we process your return, we may reduce your EIC. If the name or SSN on the child's social security card is not correct, call the Social Security Administration at 800-772-1213.
- If you have a child who meets the conditions to be your qualifying child for purposes of claiming the EIC, but that child doesn't have an SSN as defined in the instructions for Form 1040, line 27, see the instructions.

⚠ CAUTION
- *You can't claim the EIC for a child who didn't live with you for more than half of the year.*
- *If your child doesn't have an SSN as defined in the instructions for Form 1040, line 27, see the instructions.*
- *If you take the EIC even though you are not eligible, you may not be allowed to take the credit for up to 10 years. See the instructions for details.*
- *It will take us longer to process your return and issue your refund if you do not fill in all lines that apply for each qualifying child.*

Qualifying Child Information	Child 1		Child 2		Child 3	
1 Child's name If you have more than three qualifying children, you have to list only three to get the maximum credit.	First name	Last name	First name	Last name	First name	Last name
2 Child's SSN The child must have an SSN as defined in the instructions for Form 1040, line 27, unless the child was born and died in 2022 or you are claiming the self-only EIC (see instructions). If your child was born and died in 2022 and did not have an SSN, enter "Died" on this line and attach a copy of the child's birth certificate, death certificate, or hospital medical records showing a live birth.						
3 Child's year of birth	Year ____ If born after 2003 and the child is younger than you (or your spouse, if filing jointly), skip lines 4a and 4b; go to line 5.		Year ____ If born after 2003 and the child is younger than you (or your spouse, if filing jointly), skip lines 4a and 4b; go to line 5.		Year ____ If born after 2003 and the child is younger than you (or your spouse, if filing jointly), skip lines 4a and 4b; go to line 5.	
4a Was the child under age 24 at the end of 2022, a student, and younger than you (or your spouse, if filing jointly)?	☐ Yes. Go to line 5.	☐ No. Go to line 4b.	☐ Yes. Go to line 5.	☐ No. Go to line 4b.	☐ Yes. Go to line 5.	☐ No. Go to line 4b.
b Was the child permanently and totally disabled during any part of 2022?	☐ Yes. Go to line 5.	☐ No. The child is not a qualifying child.	☐ Yes. Go to line 5.	☐ No. The child is not a qualifying child.	☐ Yes. Go to line 5.	☐ No. The child is not a qualifying child.
5 Child's relationship to you (for example, son, daughter, grandchild, niece, nephew, eligible foster child, etc.)						
6 Number of months child lived with you in the United States during 2022 • If the child lived with you for more than half of 2022 but less than 7 months, enter "7." • If the child was born or died in 2022 and your home was the child's home for more than half the time he or she was alive during 2022, enter "12."	____ months Do not enter more than 12 months.		____ months Do not enter more than 12 months.		____ months Do not enter more than 12 months.	

For Paperwork Reduction Act Notice, see your tax return instructions.   Cat. No. 13339M   Schedule EIC (Form 1040) 2022

The next chapter familiarizes you with form 8880 when Savers Credits may apply.

MONEY WITH AMY SERIES

SELF-EMPLOYED TAXES:
Unleashing Schedule C Deductions

Form 8880 will only apply if your income meets the eligibility guidelines.

I mentioned above that I have seen this tax credit happen as a surprise one-time occurrence in a year with large losses and transitions into entrepreneurship that deflate income in a single tax year.

When all those tax dominoes I mentioned above fall in a specific net taxable income level sequence, this tax credit is triggered for taxpayers who have never received it before, it is a gift.

I tell my clients never count on this refund ever happening to you again.

Why?

Circumstances, your taxable income, and tax laws change. Here today could easily be gone tomorrow for this windfall.

Form 8880

Department of the Treasury
Internal Revenue Service

Credit for Qualified Retirement Savings Contributions

Attach to Form 1040, 1040-SR, or 1040-NR.
Go to *www.irs.gov/Form8880* for the latest information.

OMB No. 1545-0074

2022

Attachment
Sequence No. **54**

Name(s) shown on return

Your social security number

⚠ **CAUTION**

You **cannot** take this credit if **either** of the following applies.

- The amount on Form 1040, 1040-SR, or 1040-NR, line 11, is more than $34,000 ($51,000 if head of household; $68,000 if married filing jointly).
- The person(s) who made the qualified contribution or elective deferral (**a**) was born after January 1, 2005; (**b**) is claimed as a dependent on someone else's 2022 tax return; or (**c**) was a **student** (see instructions).

		(a) You	(b) Your spouse
1	Traditional and Roth IRA contributions, and ABLE account contributions by the designated beneficiary for 2022. **Do not** include rollover contributions **1**		
2	Elective deferrals to a 401(k) or other qualified employer plan, voluntary employee contributions, and 501(c)(18)(D) plan contributions for 2022 (see instructions) . . **2**		
3	Add lines 1 and 2 . . . . **3**		
4	Certain distributions received **after** 2019 and **before** the due date (including extensions) of your 2022 tax return (see instructions). If married filing jointly, include **both** spouses' amounts in **both** columns. See instructions for an exception . . . **4**		
5	Subtract line 4 from line 3. If zero or less, enter -0- **5**		
6	In each column, enter the **smaller** of line 5 or $2,000 . . . . **6**		

7	Add the amounts on line 6. If zero, **stop**; you can't take this credit	**7**	
8	Enter the amount from Form 1040, 1040-SR, or 1040-NR, line 11* **8**		
9	Enter the applicable decimal amount from the table below.		

If line 8 is—		And your filing status is—		
Over—	But not over—	Married filing jointly	Head of household	Single, Married filing separately, or Qualifying surviving spouse
		Enter on line 9—		
---	$20,500	0.5	0.5	0.5
$20,500	$22,000	0.5	0.5	0.2
$22,000	$30,750	0.5	0.5	0.1
$30,750	$33,000	0.5	0.2	0.1
$33,000	$34,000	0.5	0.1	0.1
$34,000	$41,000	0.5	0.1	0.0
$41,000	$44,000	0.2	0.1	0.0
$44,000	$51,000	0.1	0.1	0.0
$51,000	$68,000	0.1	0.0	0.0
$68,000	---	0.0	0.0	0.0

9 x 0 .

Note: If line 9 is zero, **stop**; you can't take this credit.

10	Multiply line 7 by line 9	**10**	
11	Limitation based on tax liability. Enter the amount from the Credit Limit Worksheet in the instructions	**11**	
12	**Credit for qualified retirement savings contributions.** Enter the **smaller** of line 10 or line 11 here and on Schedule 3 (Form 1040), line 4	**12**	

* See Pub. 590-A for the amount to enter if you claim any exclusion or deduction for foreign earned income, foreign housing, or income from Puerto Rico or for bona fide residents of American Samoa.

For Paperwork Reduction Act Notice, see your tax return instructions.

Cat. No. 33394D

Form **8880** (2022)

The next chapter familiarizes you with the Schedule SE where your net business income is used to calculate the amount of Social Security taxes you will owe.

MONEY WITH AMY SERIES

SELF-EMPLOYED TAXES:
Unleashing Schedule C Deductions

<u>Schedule SE</u> (A copy of the form is inserted at the end of this chapter for reference.)

The amount of Social Security taxes is calculated here that will flow to the 1040 form line 23 amount that is taken from the Schedule 2 line 4.

Remember I told you that all tax entries are like dominoes, they show up somewhere else or are part of a different calculation?

If you are married and you are both self-employed, you will each have your own schedule SE.

If you have more than one Schedule C business, they will all be combined into one total on this form.

How could this happen?

I have one schedule C business that is landscaping. I have a second schedule C business that has nothing to do with landscaping because I do jewelry sales on Etsy and in a couple of exclusive boutiques.

I would keep each one of my business records separate. That is just one quick example of how a person could have more than one Schedule C form for vastly different endeavors.

It is my opinion you are best served to have separate Schedule C's for your different endeavors for a variety of reasons.

One of those reasons has to do with looking at how profitable or unprofitable and endeavor is when it stands on its own two feet.

If you lump all your endeavors together it is hard to tell who is making money and who is costing you money.

You or your heirs may want to sell your business in time and having separate bookkeeping records will make the valuation and profitability of your business much easier to establish.

There is also the two out of five-year rolling profit rule that would apply to each schedule C endeavor that I already discussed in this book.

For myself employed clients I routinely include and maintain a record for each Schedule C of the profitability for the last 5-8 prior tax years to make sure we do not violate the two out of five-year rule that could jeopardize the business status and have it reclassified retroactively as a hobby.

A change of this magnitude from an audit when a business is reclassified to a hobby could create substantial new tax liabilities, penalties, and interest for the years that expense deductions were denied and removed from the return. The tax laws could easily go back three years to make these changes and there are provisions to enable this change to go back on even more years when warranted. This is a fight with the IRS you do not want to have.

This little hidden guideline is another reason having professional assistance with tax related matters can either save you money or cost you dearly for not engaging in tax related conversations before you act

Your net Schedule C earnings from line 31 will be included on this SE form and will be incorporated in the calculations if you had W2 employment and if you had more than one Schedule C.

Every year there is a maximum limit on how much of your self-employment or W2 income that you will pay in relation to your FICA taxes.

There is no limit on the amount of W2 or self-employment income that you will pay Medicare taxes on at this writing.

There is another layer of a special Medicare tax that should be explained.

The Additional Medicare Tax is a surtax imposed on certain high-income individuals to help fund Medicare. It was introduced as part of the Affordable Care Act, known as the ACA, and went into effect in 2013.

The additional Medicare Tax applies to individuals with earned income above certain thresholds.

If an individual's earned income exceeds the applicable threshold, the Additional Medicare Tax is applied to the portion of income that exceeds the threshold.

If you have an amount on Schedule 2, line 11, this additional Medicare tax applies to you and is calculated on form 8959.

It is important to note that tax rates and thresholds may change over time. To ensure you have the most up-to-date information on the Additional Medicare Tax and its rates or threshold.

I recommend consulting the official IRS website or speaking with a tax professional.

SCHEDULE SE
(Form 1040)

Department of the Treasury
Internal Revenue Service

Self-Employment Tax

Go to *www.irs.gov/ScheduleSE* for instructions and the latest information.
Attach to Form 1040, 1040-SR, or 1040-NR.

2022

Attachment
Sequence No. **17**

Name of person with self-employment income (as shown on Form 1040, 1040-SR, or 1040-NR)	Social security number of person with **self-employment** income

Part I   Self-Employment Tax

Note: If your only income subject to self-employment tax is **church employee income**, see instructions for how to report your income and the definition of church employee income.

A   If you are a minister, member of a religious order, or Christian Science practitioner **and** you filed Form 4361, but you had $400 or more of **other** net earnings from self-employment, check here and continue with Part I . . . . ☐

Skip lines 1a and 1b if you use the farm optional method in Part II. See instructions.

1a	Net farm profit or (loss) from Schedule F, line 34, and farm partnerships, Schedule K-1 (Form 1065), box 14, code A	**1a**	
b	If you received social security retirement or disability benefits, enter the amount of Conservation Reserve Program payments included on Schedule F, line 4b, or listed on Schedule K-1 (Form 1065), box 20, code AH	**1b**	( )

Skip line 2 if you use the nonfarm optional method in Part II. See instructions.

2	Net profit or (loss) from Schedule C, line 31; and Schedule K-1 (Form 1065), box 14, code A (other than farming). See instructions for other income to report or if you are a minister or member of a religious order	**2**	
3	Combine lines 1a, 1b, and 2	**3**	
4a	If line 3 is more than zero, multiply line 3 by 92.35% (0.9235). Otherwise, enter amount from line 3	**4a**	
	Note: If line 4a is less than $400 due to Conservation Reserve Program payments on line 1b, see instructions.		
b	If you elect one or both of the optional methods, enter the total of lines 15 and 17 here	**4b**	
c	Combine lines 4a and 4b. If less than $400, **stop**; you don't owe self-employment tax. **Exception:** If less than $400 and you had **church employee income**, enter -0- and continue	**4c**	
5a	Enter your **church employee income** from Form W-2. See instructions for definition of church employee income	**5a**		
b	Multiply line 5a by 92.35% (0.9235). If less than $100, enter -0-	**5b**	
6	Add lines 4c and 5b	**6**	
7	Maximum amount of combined wages and self-employment earnings subject to social security tax or the 6.2% portion of the 7.65% railroad retirement (tier 1) tax for 2022	**7**	147,000
8a	Total social security wages and tips (total of boxes 3 and 7 on Form(s) W-2) and railroad retirement (tier 1) compensation. If $147,000 or more, skip lines 8b through 10, and go to line 11	**8a**		
b	Unreported tips subject to social security tax from Form 4137, line 10 . . .	**8b**		
c	Wages subject to social security tax from Form 8919, line 10 . . .	**8c**		
d	Add lines 8a, 8b, and 8c	**8d**	
9	Subtract line 8d from line 7. If zero or less, enter -0- here and on line 10 and go to line 11 . . .	**9**	
10	Multiply the **smaller** of line 6 or line 9 by 12.4% (0.124)	**10**	
11	Multiply line 6 by 2.9% (0.029)	**11**	
12	**Self-employment tax.** Add lines 10 and 11. Enter here and on **Schedule 2 (Form 1040), line 4**	**12**	
13	**Deduction for one-half of self-employment tax.** Multiply line 12 by 50% (0.50). Enter here and on **Schedule 1 (Form 1040), line 15**	**13**		

Part II   Optional Methods To Figure Net Earnings (see instructions)

Farm Optional Method. You may use this method **only** if **(a)** your gross farm income[1] wasn't more than $9,060, **or (b)** your net farm profits[2] were less than $6,540.

14	Maximum income for optional methods	**14**	6,040
15	Enter the **smaller** of: two-thirds (⅔) of gross farm income[1] (not less than zero) **or** $6,040. Also, include this amount on line 4b above	**15**	

Nonfarm Optional Method. You may use this method **only** if **(a)** your net nonfarm profits[3] were less than $6,540 and also less than 72.189% of your gross nonfarm income,[4] **and (b)** you had net earnings from self-employment of at least $400 in 2 of the prior 3 years. **Caution:** You may use this method no more than five times.

16	Subtract line 15 from line 14	**16**	
17	Enter the **smaller** of: two-thirds (⅔) of gross nonfarm income[4] (not less than zero) **or** the amount on line 16. Also, include this amount on line 4b above	**17**	

[1] From Sch. F, line 9; and Sch. K-1 (Form 1065), box 14, code B.
[2] From Sch. F, line 34; and Sch. K-1 (Form 1065), box 14, code A – minus the amount you would have entered on line 1b had you not used the optional method.
[3] From Sch. C, line 31; and Sch. K-1 (Form 1065), box 14, code A.
[4] From Sch. C, line 7; and Sch. K-1 (Form 1065), box 14, code C.

For Paperwork Reduction Act Notice, see your tax return instructions.   Cat. No. 11358Z   Schedule SE (Form 1040) 2022

The next chapter familiarizes you with the QBI deduction calculations.

MONEY WITH AMY SERIES

SELF-EMPLOYED TAXES:
Unleashing Schedule C Deductions

<u>Form 8995</u> (A copy of the form is inserted at the end of this chapter for reference.)

The QBI deduction is calculated on form 8995 and reported as a deduction, when it applies on the 1040 Line 13.

If you have a profit when all entries are compiled, you have a good chance of being eligible for this extra deduction to reduce your gross taxable income on the 1040 line 13.

It is important to note that if you have rental properties or other eligible business endeavors reported elsewhere on your tax return, those amounts may be included on this form too.

We are not talking about rental properties or other business endeavors in this book or form discussion.

You should be aware that other endeavors with their individual profits and losses may end up on the QBI form with your self-employment profits.

If you have losses when all entries are compiled, there will be no QBI deduction.

Qualified Business Income Deduction
Simplified Computation

Attach to your tax return.

Go to *www.irs.gov/Form8995* for instructions and the latest information.

OMB No. 1545-2294

2022

Attachment
Sequence No. **55**

Name(s) shown on return

Your taxpayer identification number

Note. *You can claim the qualified business income deduction **only** if you have qualified business income from a qualified trade or business, real estate investment trust dividends, publicly traded partnership income, or a domestic production activities deduction passed through from an agricultural or horticultural cooperative. See instructions.*

Use this form if your taxable income, before your qualified business income deduction, is at or below $170,050 ($340,100 if married filing jointly), and you aren't a patron of an agricultural or horticultural cooperative.

1	(a) Trade, business, or aggregation name	(b) Taxpayer identification number	(c) Qualified business income or (loss)
i			
ii			
iii			
iv			
v			

2	Total qualified business income or (loss). Combine lines 1i through 1v, column (c)	**2**		
3	Qualified business net (loss) carryforward from the prior year	**3**	( )	
4	Total qualified business income. Combine lines 2 and 3. If zero or less, enter -0-	**4**		
5	Qualified business income component. Multiply line 4 by 20% (0.20)			**5**
6	Qualified REIT dividends and publicly traded partnership (PTP) income or (loss) (see instructions)	**6**		
7	Qualified REIT dividends and qualified PTP (loss) carryforward from the prior year	**7**	( )	
8	Total qualified REIT dividends and PTP income. Combine lines 6 and 7. If zero or less, enter -0-	**8**		
9	REIT and PTP component. Multiply line 8 by 20% (0.20)			**9**
10	Qualified business income deduction before the income limitation. Add lines 5 and 9			**10**
11	Taxable income before qualified business income deduction (see instructions)	**11**		
12	Net capital gain (see instructions)	**12**		
13	Subtract line 12 from line 11. If zero or less, enter -0-	**13**		
14	Income limitation. Multiply line 13 by 20% (0.20)			**14**
15	Qualified business income deduction. Enter the smaller of line 10 or line 14. Also enter this amount on the applicable line of your return (see instructions)			**15**
16	Total qualified business (loss) carryforward. Combine lines 2 and 3. If greater than zero, enter -0-			**16** ( )
17	Total qualified REIT dividends and PTP (loss) carryforward. Combine lines 6 and 7. If greater than zero, enter -0-			**17** ( )

For Privacy Act and Paperwork Reduction Act Notice, see instructions.   Cat. No. 37806C   Form **8995** (2022)

The next chapter we wrap up what you have learned.

CHAPTER 35

What else are you missing on your tax returns?

MONEY WITH AMY SERIES

SELF-EMPLOYED TAXES:
Unleashing Schedule C Deductions

Could there be more tax-saving opportunities you are missing, certainly there are!

It all depends on your unique dynamics and willingness to structure your affairs to your tax advantage.

We are scratching the surface here, even if I scratched a little deeply on specific tax form lines, there is always more you have not learned about, or implemented yet.

In time, you may want to consider Forming an LLC or S Corporation: Depending on your business structure and income level, forming a Limited Liability Company (LLC) or an S Corporation may provide potential tax advantages. Consult with a tax professional to determine if this is a beneficial option for your specific situation.

You may have already formed an entity and had no idea of the tax consequences of the titling you chose.

Keep detailed records!

Maintaining accurate and organized records of your income and expenses is crucial for maximizing your deductions and minimizing tax liabilities.

Utilize accounting software or consult with an accountant to ensure your records are complete and in order.

One struggle I see adults who try to self-prepare taxes to try to save a little money suffer with is staying informed and up to date about tax law changes.

Tax laws and regulations are subject to change constantly.

It is essential to stay updated on any modifications that may have an impact on your self-employment and personal income taxes.

Regularly review reliable sources of tax information (assuming you have the time to do this on top of everything else you juggle) or consult with a qualified tax professional throughout the year to ensure you remain compliant and take advantage of any new tax-saving opportunities.

The choice is up to you. I repeat, you can save thousands of dollars in taxes annually with the right strategic help.

Or you can choose to pay more in taxes than you need to by foolishly refusing to get qualified, professional help in this lifelong business-related area.

It should be said that at times your growing business situation may outgrow your tax professional or bookkeepers' knowledge base. It happens more frequently than you may realize.

Remember, every tax professional designs their office operations to suit their business goals.

One office may prefer to do simple returns and you need more complex help.

Another office may want to only put the numbers on the pages you give them with little or no discussion about what deductions may be missing to crank out multiple returns as quickly as possible in an abbreviated time span.

Another firm may be very initiative taking about helping you. You should listen!

I want to defend one part of your team that rarely gets credit for the work they do.

Your bookkeeper.

Keep in mind your bookkeeper is not a tax professional or financial advisor.

It is not fair to expect them to be.

Their job is to record the numbers correctly to be able to compile profit and loss reports and other related tasks to enable you to pay taxes, deduct expenses, and look at balance sheets. Period.

My advice is to reach out if you need help sooner rather than later when structuring your income and business expenses to your advantage.

This may be the most lifetime financially beneficial book you read this year.

A word of advice, never get too tax comfortable.

Circumstances and tax laws change constantly.

Just because you did it this way last year, does not mean it will always be the best way to do it in the years to come.

Secure professional tax help without waiting another day and spending another tax year paying more taxes than you should owe!

When it comes to making wise choices with your resources, I cast my vote for you to take steps that allow you to keep more of the money you earn starting right now!

If you would like to schedule a discovery call with me, you can use the booking link here:

https://calendly.com/amyroseherrick/15min

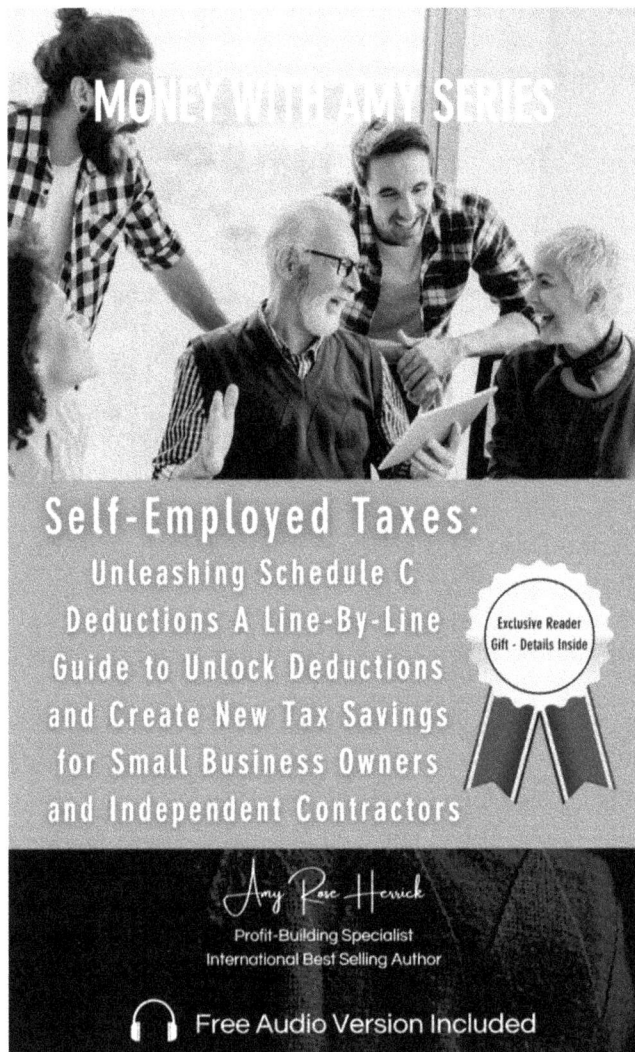

MONEY WITH AMY SERIES

Self-Employed Taxes: Unleashing Schedule C Deductions A Line-By-Line Guide to Unlock Deductions and Create New Tax Savings for Small Business Owners and Independent Contractors

Exclusive Reader Gift - Details Inside

Amy Rose Herrick

Profit-Building Specialist
International Best Selling Author

🎧 Free Audio Version Included

THANK YOU FOR READING MY BOOK!

As a thank-you, we'd love to send you a free bonus book- not for sale anywhere else. Just email us at INFO@AmyRoseHerrick.com with "Bonus Book Request" in the subject line. You'll receive your exclusive gift directly by email.

Loved the book? We'd be grateful for your honest review on Amazon— but the bonus is yours either way.

ACKNOWLEDGMENTS

Without the support of many over the years, I could not be the person I am today. I know I will forget to thank someone, but it was not my intention to do so.

To my family, who do not always understand me, but love me anyway, you mean the world to me.

To friends and colleagues who support my professional talents and literary dreams, I wish you continued success in your endeavors.

To my talented VA team who helped me to have the finished content in print form, may your dreams come true too.

To the online writing groups from around the world on Zoom meetings where we encouraged each other in the manuscript writing processes, I did it and so can you!

To my clients and live audiences who helped me learn so much about this topic with the sharing of their finances, life stories of successes and failures for me to give guidance to you today, thank you for allowing me to have a positive impact on your lives.

To my mentors, I promise to pay it forward.

To my draft version reviewers with all the encouragement to get this finished quickly, thank you.

And finally, to all the ones behind the scenes we take for granted that make websites, online ordering, eBooks, printing, shipping, and delivery possible for us all…a heartfelt thank you for being a part of my world every day.

About the Author

Amy Rose Herrick, ChFC, is an extraordinary author and financial expert dedicated to transforming lives while empowering individuals and businesses to achieve unparalleled financial success.

She has masterminded remarkable solutions that take 15 minutes or less to understand and implement.

Her expertise shines brightest creating personalized, comprehensive plans that streamline costs, provide peace of mind, and secure wealth for future generations.

Bid farewell to financial stress while embracing your legacy that will endure the test of time.

Amy, your personal wealth building guide, unleashes the power within your resources.

Complex resource management problems are transformed into easy step by step solutions.

Using groundbreaking methodology, Amy empowers individuals, business owners, and families alike.

Entrepreneurs flock to Amy for clear, actionable tutorials on building more profitable businesses. Under her guidance, ventures can thrive like never before, unlocking their true potential for financial success.

As a fiduciary, Chartered Financial Consultant, and tax professional, Amy has mastered the art of optimizing resources.

Yet, her achievements do not stop there. She is a #1 Best Selling Author, captivating speaker, talented artist, and a dedicated force in community service.

With over three decades of experience, including more than 25 years in the Securities industry, Amy possesses an impressive array of qualifications and expertise. She equips you with the tools to experience lasting financial freedom, providing a transformative journey unlike any other.

Be prepared for the launch of a series of game-changing books and captivating YouTube videos titled "Money With Amy."

Her dynamic and easy-to-understand content will empower you to strategically structure your resources for the benefit of your family and businesses.

Amy Rose Herrick's list of remarkable accomplishments is truly awe-inspiring. From being named Small Business of the Year to being a #1 Best Selling Author, a National Geographic 'Chasing Genius' Finalist, and even teaching a gorilla named Max, Amy's impact is undeniable.

Clients can expect an unforgettable, life-changing experience with Amy Rose Herrick, one that simply cannot be replicated elsewhere.

Currently residing by the sea in the breathtaking US Virgin Islands, Amy continues to live a life of abundance while sharing her wealth of knowledge with the world.

For Additional Information & Resources

Visit Amy's website: **www.AmyRoseHerrick.com**

Email: **Amy@AmyRoseHerrick.com**

Book a 15-minute Zoom based discovery call to discuss becoming a client for comprehensive financial planning or business profit building assistance at:

https://calendly.com/amyroseherrick/15min

Follow Amy on Facebook

https://www.facebook.com/AmyRoseHerrickProfitBuildingSpecialist

Listen to Amy's Podcast appearances on a variety of topics:

https://www.listennotes.com/search/?q=amy%20rose%20herrick&sort_by_date=0&scope=episode&offset=0&language=Any%20language&len_min=0

Read Amy's articles on Medium at : https://medium.com/search?q=amy+rose+herrick

Reach out to Amy at Amy@AmyRoseHerrick.com to inquire about booking Amy to be on your show as a guest or for autographed copies.

Watch one of Amy's full length financial literacy building educational videos on YouTube

https://www.youtube.com/@amyprofitspecialist

Linked in: https://www.linkedin.com/in/amyroseherrick/

Instagram: amyroseherrick

Alignable: https://www.alignable.com/christiansted-vi/amy-rose-herrick-chfc-americas-profit-building-specialist

Amazon all current titles for sale link:

https://www.amazon.com/s?k=amy+rose+herrick&crid=SGL1PHGTWZS5&sprefix=amy+rose+herrick%2Caps%2C179&ref=nb_sb_noss_1

Other titles available now, or coming soon, in the MONEY WITH AMY SERIES that may be of interest to you:

MONEY WITH AMY SERIES

The Profitable Entrepreneur:

16 Ways to Retrain Entrepreneurs Using Mindset, Time Management, Leveraging Your Resources and Enjoying More Business Travel Inexpensively

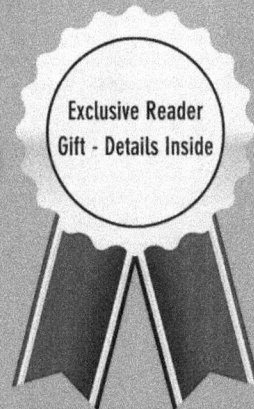

Exclusive Reader Gift - Details Inside

Amy Rose Herrick

Profit-Building Specialist
International Best Selling Author

🎧 Free Audio Version Included

MONEY WITH AMY SERIES

Building your foundation: ENTREPRENEURIAL MISTAKES TO AVOID

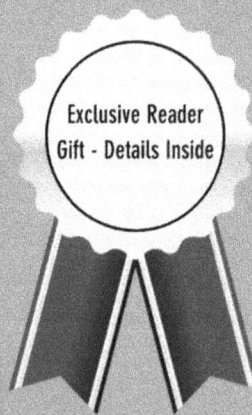

Exclusive Reader Gift - Details Inside

Amy Rose Herrick

Profit-Building Specialist
International Best Selling Author

Free Audio Version Included

MONEY WITH AMY SERIES

KNOWING YOUR LIFE PARTNER:

25 QUESTIONS TO ASK AND ANSWER (FOR COUPLES IN THEIR FIRST LONG TERM RELATIONSHIP)

Exclusive Reader
Gift - Details Inside

Amy Rose Herrick

Profit-Building Specialist
International Best Selling Author

Free Audio Version Included

MONEY WITH AMY SERIES

REMARRIAGE:
25 QUESTIONS TO ASK
AND ANSWER
BEFORE REMARRIAGE

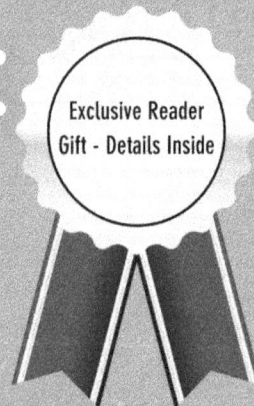

Exclusive Reader Gift - Details Inside

Amy Rose Herrick

Profit-Building Specialist
International Best Selling Author

Free Audio Version Included

MONEY WITH AMY SERIES

MARRIAGE AFTER RETIREMENT:
25 QUESTIONS TO ASK AND ANSWER BEFORE YOU MARRY

Exclusive Reader Gift - Details Inside

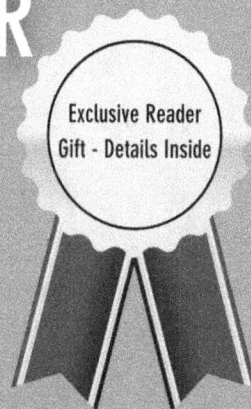

Amy Rose Herrick

Profit-Building Specialist
International Best Selling Author

Free Audio Version Included

MONEY WITH AMY SERIES

Protecting Your Health and Wealth:
Your Step-by-Step Guide for Multi-Generational Medical Planning

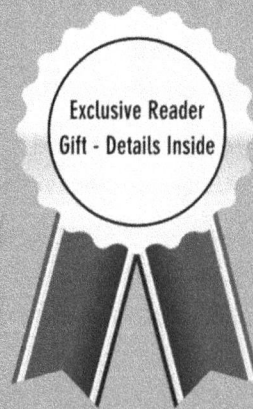

Exclusive Reader Gift - Details Inside

Amy Rose Herrick

Profit-Building Specialist
International Best Selling Author

Free Audio Version Included